USING THE LIBRARY: The Card Catalog

Charles I. Bradshaw with Marvin E. Wiggins and Blaine Hall

A project of the
Instructional Development Program and the
Instructional Research and Development Department,
Instructional Services Division
Brigham Young University

Brigham Young University Press

Library of Congress Catalog Card Number: 71-175298
ISBN 0-8425-0817-1
Brigham Young University Press, Provo, Utah 84601
© By Brigham Young University Press. All rights reserved
Printed in the United States of America
Printing Code 9-71 10M 95165

The authors wish to express special thanks to Dr. M. David Merrill of the Instructional Research and Development Department and Dr. R. Irwin Goodman of the Instructional Development Program of BYU for their critical comments and guidance in the development of this instructional package. Further thanks are given to Darwin Hayes of the BYU English Department; and special thanks to Lamia Hooper for her help with the visual material.

ACKNOWLEDGMENTS

CONTENTS

Preliminary research conducted on undergraduate students at a major university showed that those students tested averaged only 32 percent correct on their pretest knowledge of the workings of the library card catalog. This card catalog program text has been designed to help the student learn the use of the card catalog and to use it faster and more effectively.

The program deals with six aspects of the card catalog: (1) filing rules, (2) call numbers, (3) cross-referencing, (4) author, title, and subject cards, (5) tracings, and (6) the book *Subject Headings Used in the Dictionary Catalogs of the Library of Congress*.

There are three main divisions of the material presented: (1) pretest, (2) workbook, and (3) posttest. The tests are designed to be self-administered and self-scored. The student should take the pretest and grade it himself; it will show in which of the six areas of the card catalog he needs instructional help. The student then should follow the instruction outlined in each of the critical areas as indicated by the pretest results.

The student should spend as much or as little time in instruction as is felt necessary before taking the posttest. The posttest is essentially the same as the pretest. The score of the pretest may be compared with that of the posttest, and the student can measure his actual learning gain. It was shown from the research conducted during the development of this program that there is a close correlation between the students' score on the posttest (84 percent average performance) and their ability to actually use the card catalog.

Step 1
Student should turn to the Pretest and read the instructions.

PRETEST

PRETEST INSTRUCTIONS

The library card catalog pretest is designed to help you see more clearly those areas of the card catalog in which you need instruction. The areas it deals with are (1) filing rules, (2) call numbers, (3) cross-referencing, (4) author, title, and subject cards, (5) tracings, and (6) the book *Subject Headings Used in the Dictionary Catalogs of the Library of Congress.*

The following options are suggested for the pretest. Choose the one that fits your needs and proceed from there.

Option 1. If you feel you know little about any of the six areas listed above, skip the pretest and go directly to Step 2 below.

Option 2. If you feel you know something about some of the areas but not about others, take the pretest. It will give you specific direction as to what you need to study. When you finish the pretest, grade it (you will find the key at the end of the test), then proceed with Step 2 below.

Option 3. If you feel you know quite a bit about the card catalog, take the pretest anyway. You may be surprised. If not, so much the better. You'll have more of an idea of what to expect on the posttest. When you finish the pretest, grade it, then proceed with Step 2 below.

Step 2
Turn to the Workbook sections and follow the directions.

Directions: Select the <u>one best</u> answer for each of the following questions.

1. To find in the card catalog the book *21 Delightful Ways to Commit Suicide* you would look under
   a. *Delightful*
   b. the number 21 in the number section of the card catalog
   c. the word *twenty-one* (the number 21 spelled out)
   d. Such a title would not have a title card but would, instead, be filed under the author's name or subject heading
   e. I'm not sure

2. Where would the book *21 Delightful Ways to Commit Suicide* be filed in the card catalog in relation to the book *20 Elegant Ways to Cook Eel*?
   a. before
   b. after
   c. it could be either before or after with the system used at most universities
   d. I'm not sure

3. To find the book *And There Was a Great Calm* in the card catalog, you would look under
   a. *And*
   b. *There*
   c. either *a* or *b*—cards are filed both ways at most universities
   d. such a title would not have a title card but would, instead, be filed under the author's name or subject heading
   e. I'm not sure

4. The title card for the book *Onions and Their Allies* would be found filed in which tray?
   a. On c—On the r
   b. On the s—one h
   c. One i—O'Neill, E
   d. O'Neill, F—Oo
   e. I'm not sure

5. An author card for William John McCombs would be found in which tray?
   a. Comb - Comg
   b. Mazj - Meaning o
   c. M - Macaq
   d. Maccom - Maccq
   e. I'm not sure

6. An author card for James M'Astel would be found filed
   a. before McArthur and before MacFarlane
   b. after M'Aberdeen and after MacDougal
   c. before MacAuley and after MacArthur
   d. after MacMellon and before M'Ferson
   e. I'm not sure

7. The title card for the book *America's New Policy Makers* would be found in which tray?
   a. Amer - America de
   b. American e - Americains
   c. American-Amer. Art Assoc
   d. Amer. Women-Amerika
   e. I'm not sure

8. The title card for the book *St. John of the Cross* would be found filed in which tray?

a. Saill - Saint g

c. Saint pi - Saints r

b. Saint h - Saint pet

d. Stig - Stn

9. An author card for Charles William Armstrong-Jones (Armstrong-Jones is a compound last name) would be found in which tray?

a. Armenian-Armstrong, K

c. Joint, d - Jones, C

b. Armstrong, L - Arnold, B

d. Jones, R - Jonf

SECTION **2** CALL NUMBERS

Directions: For the following question, refer to the sample call number chart on the next page. Choose your answers for all three questions from the single set of choices listed below. In each case, choose the one best answer.

1. Where would you find this book?

448.242 M532f	Pei, Mario Andrew, 1901-

jt. au.

Meras, Edmond Albert, 1896
First-year French; a conversational grammar (by) Edmond A. Meras (and) Mario A. Pei. New York, Dryden Press (1950)

xxx, 500 p. 22cm. (The Dryden Press modern language publications)

a. Level 1
b. Level 2
c. Level 3
d. Level 4
e. Level 5
f. Room 407
g. Room 426
h. M'200 section of Level 4
i. I'm not sure

2. Where would you find this book?

Burns
821.671
B93
1902

Ford, Robert, 1846-1905, ed.

Burns, Robert, 1759-1796.

The poems and songs of Robert Burns, with notes and glossary. London, G. Newnes, ltd., 1902.

2p. L. iii-ixxii, 580 p. front 17 cm.

Engraved t. p.
Notes and glossary by Robert Ford.
"An essay on Burns by Thomas Carlyle": p. xvii-ixxii

a. Level 1
b. Level 2
c. Level 3
d. Level 4
e. Level 5
f. Room 407
g. Room 426
h. M'200 section of Level 4
i. I'm not sure

3. Where would you find this book?

```
Microprint        The Family Almanac.
080
Sh64

                  This work is available in this library in the Rendex
                  Micropring edition of Early American Imprints
                  published by the American Antiquarian Society.



                  This collection is arranged according to the numbers
                  in Charles Evans's American Bibliography.
```

a. Level 1
b. Level 2
c. Level 3
d. Level 4
e. Level 5
f. Room 407
g. Room 426
h. M'200 section
   of Level 4
i. I'm not sure

Sample Call Number Chart

Call Number	Level	Call Number	Level	Call Number	Level
000-049	5	160-199	4	600-649	2
050-079	1	200-299	4	650-659	1
080-099	5	M200-M299	4	660-699	2
100-129	4	300-399	1	700-799	5
130-139	1	400-499	5	800-899	5
140-149	4	500-599	2	900-999	4
150-159	1				

Symbol	Location
Americana	Rm. 407 - Special Collections
Arabic	4th Level - Stacks
Asian Collection	4th Level - Stacks
Braille	Rm. 407 - Special Collections
Burns	Rm. 407 - Special Collections
Canadian Document	2nd Level - Documents Collection
Clark	Rm. 407 - Special Collections
Cur E	1st Level - Curriculum Collection
Cur S	1st Level - Curriculum Collection
Curriculum Ref.	1st Level - Curriculum Collection
Documents Collection	2nd Level
File	Rm. 407 - Special Collections
Film	Rm. 426 - Microfilm Rm.
Filmstrip	5th Level - Desk
Grant	Rm. 407 - Special Collections
H080	Rm. 407 - Special Collections
Hafen	Rm. 407 - Special Collections
IRC	Rm. 407 - Special Collections
L. C.	Rm. 407 - Pioneer Rm.
M200-M299	4th Level
Map Collection	2nd Level
Melville	Rm. 407 - Special Collections
Microcard	Rm. 426 - Microfilm Rm.
Microfiche	Rm. 426 - Microfilm Rm.
Microprint	Rm. 426 - Microfilm Rm.
Music	5th Level
Music Research	5th Level
Phonodisc	5th Level - Listening Library
Presses	Rm. 407 - Special Collections
Rare	Rm. 407 - Special Collections
Ref.	3rd Level
Ref. 1	1st Level
Ref. 4	4th Level
Ref. 5	5th Level
Rowe	Rm. 407 - Special Collections
Sci. Ref.	2nd Level
Vault	Rm. 407 - Special Collections
Victorian	Rm. 407 - Special Collections
Welsh	4th Level - Stacks
Whitman	Rm. 407 - Special Collections

The symbols OS, f, q above or before the call number indicate oversized books shelved at the end of each major call number section.

SECTION **3** CROSS-REFERENCE CARDS

Directions: Select the <u>one best</u> answer for each of the following questions.

1. Books under the subject heading *Eel Worms* are actually filed under the subject heading *Nematoda.* How would you discover this if you did not know?
   a. when you looked up *Eel Worms,* you would find a card that reads "See Nematoda"
   b. you would need to consult the reference librarian
   c. you would need to begin checking the cross-references on some book concerning eel worms, and eventually you would run across the heading "Nematoda"
   d. you would not be able to tell in this case
   e. I'm not sure

2. The subject heading *Cream* has several title cards filed under it in the card catalog. There are other subject headings related to cream that may also be of value—such as *Milk* and *Dairy Cattle.* How would you learn of these additional subject headings?
   a. when you looked up *Cream* in the card catalog, you would find a card that reads "see also Milk, Dairy Cattle, Dairying"
   b. you would need to consult the reference librarian
   c. you would need to begin checking the cross-references on some book related to cream, and eventually you would run across the headings *Milk and Dairy Cattle.*
   d. You would not be able to tell in this case
   e. I'm not sure

SECTION **4** AUTHOR, SUBJECT, AND TITLE CARDS

Directions: Select the <u>one best</u> answer for each of the following questions.

1. The words in red at the top of some library cards indicate
   a. the subject heading
   b. the title
   c. the author
   d. an additional subject heading to which you could refer
   e. an additional book title to which you could refer
   f. none of the above
   g. I'm not sure

2. Books *about* an author are filed where in relation to books *by* him?
   a. before
   b. after
   c. in most filing systems, either before or after is acceptable
   d. I'm not sure

3. Books about the subject *wood* (e.g., *Wood and Its Uses*) are filed where in relation to books by an author named Wood (e.g., James Wood)?
   a. before
   b. after
   c. in most filing systems, either before or after is acceptable
   d. I'm not sure

14

4. Cards with the same subject heading are filed in what order in the card catalog?
   a. alphabetical order according to the first word of the title
   b. alphabetical order according to the author's last name
   c. chronologically according to the date of printing
   d. none of the above
   e. I'm not sure

5. Who is the author?

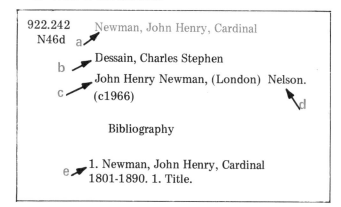

922.242 Newman, John Henry, Cardinal
N46d a.

   b   Dessain, Charles Stephen

      John Henry Newman, (London) Nelson.
c (c1966) d

      Bibliography

e 1. Newman, John Henry, Cardinal
    1801-1890. 1. Title.

a.
b.
c.
d.
e.
f. I'm not sure

6. What is the title?

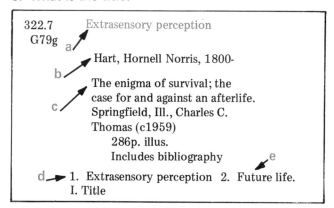

322.7 Extrasensory perception
G79g a

   b   Hart, Hornell Norris, 1800-

      The enigma of survival; the
   c case for and against an afterlife.
      Springfield, Ill., Charles C.
      Thomas (c1959)
        286p. illus.
        Includes bibliography   e

d 1. Extrasensory perception 2. Future life.
   I. Title

a.
b.
c.
d.
e.
f. I'm not sure

Directions: Select the <u>one best</u> answer for each of the following questions.

1. The tracings on a library card will refer you to additional *book* titles you can look up that are related to the one on that particular card.
   a. true   b. false   c. I'm not sure

2. The tracings on a library card will often refer you to additional *subject headings* you can look under to find books related to the one you are looking for.
   a. true   b. false   c. I'm not sure

3. The arabic numeral(s) in the tracings on a library card
   a. indicate additional *book* titles available and related to this one
   b. indicate title and/or author cards available on that particular book
   c. both *a* and *b*
   d. indicate related subject heading cards available
   e. I'm not sure

4. The roman numeral(s) in the tracings on a library card
   a. indicate title and added entry cards that may be available on that particular book (mainly for librarians' use)
   b. indicate related subject heading cards available
   c. indicate additional *books* available and related to this one
   d. there are no roman numerals in the tracings
   e. I'm not sure

SECTION **6** SUBJECT HEADINGS IN THE LIBRARY OF CONGRESS

Directions: If you know nothing about the book <u>Subject Headings Used in the Dictionary Catalogs of the Library of Congress</u>, you need not answer any of the following questions.
Mark *a* for number 1.

1. I am not familiar enough with the book *Subject Headings Used in the Dictionary Catalogs of the Library of Congress* to answer the questions in this section.
   a.

2. Which of the following does the book *Subject Headings Used in the Dictionary Catalogs of the Library of Congress* help you with? (Mark *all* correct answers.)
   a. it gives you subject headings not filed in the card catalog
   b. it gives you book titles and their corresponding subject headings not otherwise found in the card catalog
   c. it helps you narrow a field of research to more specific headings
   d. it helps you expand a subject of research to include more and related subjects
   e. it gives a comprehensive list of authors, subject headings, and book titles available in the Library of Congress
   f. I'm not sure

3. An *xx* entry in the book *Subject Headings Used in the Dictionary Catalogs of the Library of Congress* indicates: (Select the *one best* answer.)
   a. a heading that will only lead back to the main heading
   b. a good but less-related heading
   c. the best heading to look up for related information
   d. a subject heading with books by the same name
   e. a heading that is not filed as listed—indicating that you must refer to another reference book for the correct listing
   f. I'm not sure

4. An *x* entry indicates: (Select the *one best* answer.)

   a. a heading that will only lead back to the main heading
   b. a good but less-related heading
   c. the best heading to look up for related information
   d. a subject heading with books by the same name
   e. a heading that is not filed as listed—indicating that you must refer to another reference book for the correct listing
   f. I'm not sure

5. An *sa* entry indicates: (Select the *one best* answer.)

    a. an article in the journal "Scientific American"

    b. a "series of articles" are available in various journals

    c. a "scientific article" only

    d. a "social-science article" only

    e. "see also"

    f. I'm not sure

Grading your pretest   Your answers are either entirely correct or entirely wrong. For example, if c, d, and e are all part of the correct response, you need to have all letters (and no more than that) to get it correct. Don't cheat yourself. Sometimes just an extra letter or one left out indicates whether or not you understand the principle involved.

**PRETEST
ANSWER KEY**

Section 1

1. c
2. b
3. a
4. d
5. d
6. c
7. d
8. b
9. b

Section 2

1. e
2. f
3. g

Section 3

1. a
2. a

Section 4

1. a
2. b
3. b
4. b
5. b
6. c

Section 5

1. b
2. a
3. d
4. a

Section 6

1.
2. a, c, d
3. b
4. a
5. e

There are six instructional sections in the workbook. Each contains a **Program** and a **Summary,** illustrated figures, questions for you to answer, and key answers. The Program provides a course of study which when pursued should better help you learn the fundamental concepts involved in each section. When following the Program, write your answers to the questions in the spaces provided on the workbook pages (if you intend to resell this text, make your responses on a separate piece of paper). The answers for each question and a brief explanation are found by curling the page over. When you answer a question, you should turn to the answer immediately, to check your progress. The Summary should be read if you desire to obtain a brief statement of facts.

Read the following options and select the one that best applies to you.

Option 1. If you did not take the pretest because you felt you needed all of the instruction, or if you took the pretest but missed more than ten questions, begin with the Program of workbook section 1. Proceed through the entire series of six program sections. When you have spent as much time in instruction as you feel is necessary, proceed with Step 3 below.

Option 2. If you did well on the pretest (if you answered correctly at least eighteen of the twenty-eight questions possible), you probably will do well with just the Summary, which follows each section. However, if studying just the Summary to each of the six sections does not leave you with a confident working knowledge in a particular area or areas of the card catalog, feel free to return and study the Program, answering the workbook questions for these critical areas where you need to be better informed. When you have spent as much time in this instruction as you feel is necessary, proceed with Step 3 below.

Step 3
Take the posttest and review any sections on which you still do poorly.

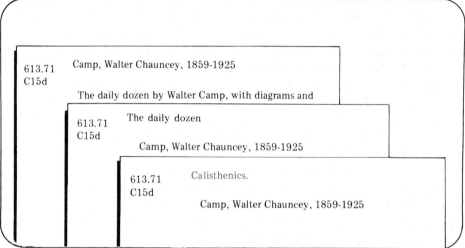

613.71
C15d   Camp, Walter Chauncey, 1859-1925

         The daily dozen by Walter Camp, with diagrams and

613.71   The daily dozen
C15d

         Camp, Walter Chauncey, 1859-1925

613.71   Calisthenics.
C15d

         Camp, Walter Chauncey, 1859-1925

FIG. 1

FIG. 2

Lattam, Peter

FIG. 3

SECTION **1** PROGRAM FILING RULES

The primary purpose of the workbook instructional sections is to help you find what you are looking for in the library card catalog and to find it easier and faster. This can be done by making you aware of a few simple rules.

The first rule states that everything in the card catalog is listed on cards and filed in alphabetical order.

Alphabetical Order

Figure 1 refers to the three main kinds of cards found in the card catalog: author cards, title cards, and subject cards. For any given book there are usually these three kinds of cards in the card catalog. You can find the reference or *call number* for books by looking up any or all of these cards. (Other scripts in this series go into detail about the characteristics of these three kinds of cards.)

At times when you have used the library before, you may have noticed that each tray of cards in the card catalog is labeled. Each label consists of letters of the alphabet indicating the first card in the tray and the last card. Figure 2 shows one of the trays. In this tray you would find author cards, subject heading cards, and title cards that begin with the letters LAUE and that go through LAUV. You would not find a card for the name LAUDON nor for the heading LAVA. Be sure that you understand why. The reason is that the letters of this tray do not begin soon enough to pick up LAUDON nor do they go far enough to include LAVA.

Tray Filing

Question 1
Refer to the name in figure 3.
Would this name be found in the tray in figure 2?

_____

Question 2
Would you find the card for Peter Lattam in the tray before or after the tray illustrated in figure 2?

_____

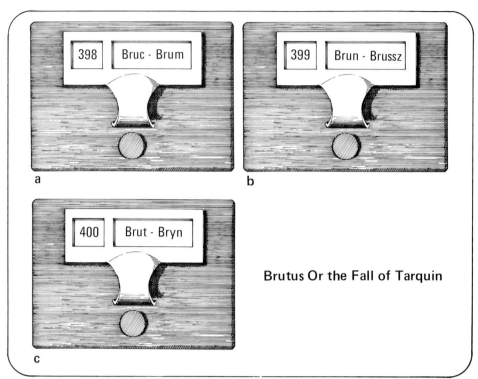

Brutus Or the Fall of Tarquin

FIG. 4

Answer 1
No. *LAT of the name Lattam comes before LAUE, which is the first card in this tray.*

Answer 2
It would be found in a tray before the one in figure 2.

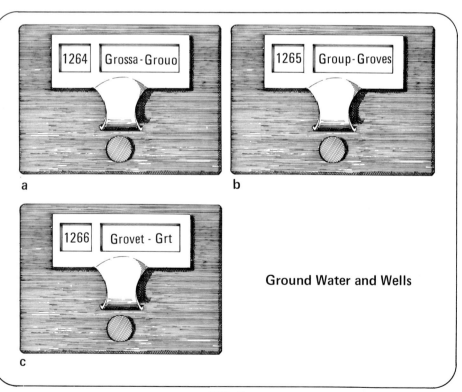

Ground Water and Wells

FIG. 5

Question 3
Look at figure 4. The fronts of three card trays as you would see them in the card catalog are shown here. In which tray (a, b, or c) would you find a title card for the book Brutus or the Fall of Tarquin?

_____

Question 4
Look at figure 5. Which tray (a, b, or c) would hold the title card for the book Ground Water and Wells?

_____

FIG. 6

A Beautiful Day in Spring

FIG. 7

But Doctor, I Don't Want to Die

FIG. 8

WORD BY WORD

LETTER BY LETTER

FIG. 9

WORD BY WORD	LETTER BY LETTER
New Jersey	Newark
New York	New Jersey
Newark	Newspapers
Newspapers	Newton
Newton	New York
Next to Valour	Next to Valour

FIG. 10

The second rule you need to know is illustrated in figure 6. It states that cards are filed in the catalog by the first word of the title, *unless* the first word is an article — that is *a*, *an*, or *the*.

First Word

Question 5

If you were looking up the title The Young Lion*, which word would you look under in the card catalog?*

_____

Questions 6 and 7

Under which word would you look for the title given in figure 7? Which word is disregarded by the filing clerk in this title?

_____

_____

Question 8

Look at figure 8. What word would you look under in the card catalog for the illustrated title?

_____

Question 9

What word would you look under for the title And Then There Were None?

_____

Figure 9 introduces the third rule. It illustrates that in *most* card catalog systems cards are filed word by word — not letter by letter. For example, look at figure 10. Study these two filing systems and note the differences in them. It can be seen in the first list that in word-by-word filing all words beginning with the word *new* are filed before words that attach another letter to the word *new* — such as *Newark*. Letter-by-letter filing as shown in the second list takes no notice of where one word stops and the next begins.

Word-By-Word

FIG. 11

a.	b.
New Amsterdam	New Amsterdam
Newark	New England
New England	New Wives for Old
Newman	Newark
New Wives for Old	Newman

FIG. 12

a. I Met a Man
b. Im Wandel der Jahre
c. Image Books
d. Images of America
e. Imaginary Conversations
f. In an Unknown Land
g. In the Days of Giants
h. Inca

12. Image of America
13. Imagism and the Imagists

FIG. 13

Question 10

Look at figure 11. Which would you find filed first in a word-by-word system, New Zoramford *or* Newton?

_____

Question 11

Look at figure 12. Which list is an example of word-by-word filing, column a *or column* b?

_____

Question 12

Look at the titles in figure 13. You will note that several of the lines are lettered. At the bottom of the figure are two numbered headings, 12 and 13. They correspond to questions 12 and 13. Look at heading number 12 and decide where you would find this heading filed among the lettered entries. Would it come between a *and* b, *between* b *and* c, *between* c *and* d, *and so forth?*

_____

Question 13

Look at heading number 13 in figure 13. Decide where you would find this heading filed among the lettered entries. Would it come between a *and* b, *between* b *and* c, *between* c *and* d, *and so forth?*

_____

Answer 10

Following the word-by-word rule, the words **New Zoramford** *come before the word* Newton.

Answer 11

b *is correct. As you can see, the word* new *has been followed all the way through before adding the* a *of* Newark.

Answer 12

For the title Image of America, *you should have said between* **c** *and* **d**. *"Image of" comes after* image books *and comes before* images.

Answer 13

It would come between **e** *and* **f**. *IMAGIS of the word* Imagism *comes after the IMAGIN of the word* Imaginary, *and it comes before the IN of* In an Unknown Land.

American before America's

FIG. 14

a. Amer - America de

b. America e - Americains

c. American - American Art

d. American women - Amerikan

e. Amerikas - Amm

America's New Song

FIG. 15

a. Twombly

b. Twopenny

c. two's company

d. Twyford

e. two years

FIG. 16

Remember: in word-by-word filing, follow one word all the way through before you start on the next word. Also, in word-by-word filing the apostrophe is dropped when filing. Look at figure 14. Under the word-by-word rule, you might think that the *s* was separate from the word *America* and, therefore, the word *America's* would come before *American*. However, this is not correct. The apostrophe is dropped, making the *s* part of the word. Therefore, *American* comes before *Americas*.

Apostrophe

Question 14
Look at figure 15. In which tray would you find the book America's New Song?

_____

Question 15
Look at figure 16. Using the word-by-word filing rule, rearrange the words given so that they are in the correct filing order. What is the new order of the letters preceding each word?

_____

St. John
Moser-Rath
Smith-Hughes
Armstrong-Jones

for example {
Dora Saint
Robert St. John
St. Augustine's Confessions

FIG. 17

Answer 14
d *is the correct answer. AMERICAN runs through tray* **d**, *and the AMERIC of America's comes before AMERIKAN, which is the last entry in the tray.*

Glass, Albert
Glass, William
Glass
Glass blowing and working
The Glass Cage
Glass House of Prejudice
Glass Through the Ages
Glasscock
Glasser

FIG. 18

Answer 15
The correct order is **e,a,b,c,d**. *The word-by-word rule places* two years, *with it TWO as one word, before the rest. Next would come TWOM of* Twombly, *TWOP of* Two-penny, *TWOS of* two's, *and finally TWY of* Twyford.

100 one hundred

204 two hundred and four

1001 one thousand and one

FIG. 19

Now, let us look at two fairly simple but important variations of the word-by-word filing rule. Look first at figure 17. Examples of compound surnames are illustrated. Such names are filed immediately *after* the simple surname and *before* subject and title headings by the same simple surname. For example, consider the name *Robert St. John* as given in the figure. *St. John* in this case is a compound surname and is consequently filed after *Dora Saint*, because the compound surname follows the simple surname in filing. However, the name *St. John* would come before *St. Augustine's Confessions*, since the compound surname is filed before subject and title cards.

The other variation is shown in figure 18. Here is illustrated an example of word-by-word filing that does not follow exactly the previously stated rules. In figure 18 all of the entries with the surname *Glass* have been filed before the subject heading *Glass* and before the title and subject cards beginning with the word *glass*. The rule then states that author cards are filed before title and subject cards of the same name.

It is important to remember that all numbers are filed as if they were spelled out. Look at figure 19. "100" reads "one hundred." "204" reads "two hundred and four." "1001" becomes "one thousand and one."

76 Trombones
63 Exciting Ways to Cook Eel

FIG. 20

109 Fun Camera Projects
108 Steps to Health

FIG. 21

One Hundred Friendly Insects
105 Friends of the Bird

FIG. 22

Hegel, Georg Wilhelm Friedrich
Heinlein, Robert A.
Hemingway, Ernest

FIG. 23

FIG. 24

Question 16
Of the two titles in figure 20, which would you find first in order in the card catalog?

_____

Question 17
In figure 21, which title would be the first entry in the tray?

_____

Question 18
Of the two titles given in figure 22, which would come first according to the word-by-word filing rule?

_____

Figure 23 illustrates the fourth important rule we need to know. Regarding author cards, the filing rules tell us to file last name first in alphabetical order. This is usually not difficult unless the last name is something like the one shown in figure 24.

Author's Last Name First

Answer 16

76 Trombones *is the correct answer. The SEV of the words* seventy-six *comes before the SIX of* sixty-three.

Answer 17

108 Steps to Health. *Eight always comes before nine— even alphabetically.*

Answer 18

105 Friends of the Bird *is the correct answer. ONE HUNDRED A of* one hundred and five *comes before ONE HUNDRED F of* one hundred friendly.

M'
Mac   Mac
Mc

FIG. 25

M'Allister or McAllen

FIG. 26

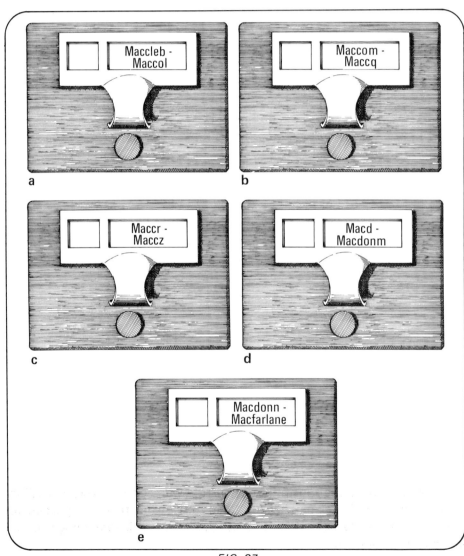

Maccleb - Maccol   a

Maccom - Maccq   b

Maccr - Maccz   c

Macd - Macdonm   d

Macdonn - Macfarlane   e

FIG. 27

The rule for such names as M'Allister is given in figure 25. It says that *M'*,   "MAC"
Mc, and *Mac* are all filed as though they were MAC.

Question 19
Figure 26 gives two authors'
names. Write which name you
would find filed first in the
card catalog.

Figure 27 illustrates the fronts of several card catalog trays. We learned
earlier that the fronts of the trays can be helpful in directing us to the proper
one. The fronts of the trays can be helpful in locating these "Mac's."

Question 20
Would you find the author's
name MacDonald *in tray*
a,b,c,d, *or* e *in figure 27?*

Question 21
In which tray in figure 27
would you find the name
Robert McClosky?

Questions 22 and 23
Of the authors' names
M'Conaughy *and* MacCune,
which would come first in the
card catalog? In which tray of
figure 27 would this first
reference be found?

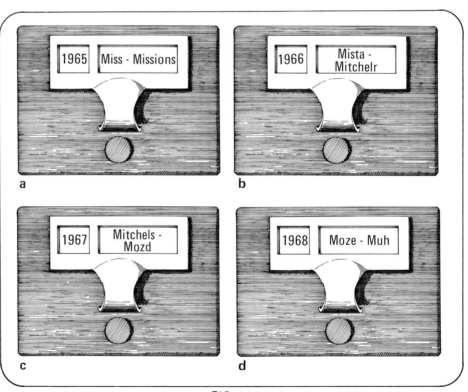

FIG. 28

St.   Saint
Dr.   Doctor
Mr.   Mister
Mrs.   Mrs.

FIG. 29

1965	Miss - Missions
a	

1966	Mista - Mitchelr
b	

1967	Mitchels - Mozd
c	

1968	Moze - Muh
d	

FIG. 30

Figure 28 depicts our fifth important rule. It is a simple rule but is some-times misunderstood. It states that abbreviations are filed as if spelled out and are considered to be a part of the title in this form. Figure 29 illustrates how this is done for several common abbreviations.

"Mrs."

You will notice in figure 29 that *Mrs.* is an exception to the abbreviation rule. If you were to look up *Mistress* in the card catalog, it would say, "see Mrs." For this abbreviation, you should look in the card catalog under the abbreviation itself.

Question 24
Referring to the trays illustrated in figure 30, in which tray (a,b,c, or d) would you find the title Mrs. Pennypacker Goes to Rome?

_____

Question 25
Referring again to the trays in figure 30, in which one would you find the title Mr. Peabody and the Mermaid?

_____

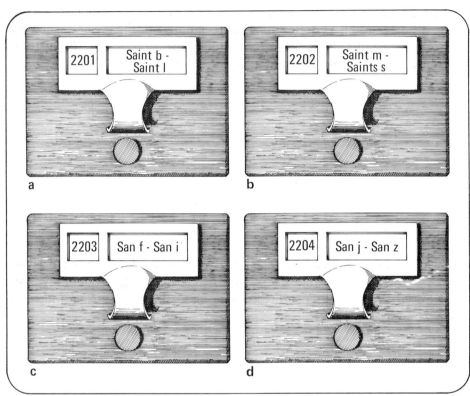

FIG. 31

Answer 24

d *is correct. Here you would find MRS of Mrs. Pennypacker Goes to Rome.*

Answer 25

b *is the correct answer. Mr. is spelled out MISTER. It would be filed between the MISTA and MITCHELR of tray b.*

1. Author cards before title and subject cards

Works **by** an author would be filed in the tray before works **about** him.

Burroughs, Edgar Rice   **before**   Burroughs, Edgar Rice

2. Pseudonyms (fictitious names)

Books are listed under the author's real name with a cross reference from his pseudonym if he has one.

Padgett, Lewis (pseud.)
see
Kuttner, Henry

3. Identical Names

Identical Names are filed by date of birth.

Leiber, Fritz, 1883-1949
Leiber, Fritz, 1910-

FIG. 32

Question 26
Which title would you find filed first in the card catalog—St. Joan of Arc or San Louis Obispo County History?

_____

Question 27
In which of the trays illustrated in figure 31 would you find the first filed reference card from question 26?

_____

Figure 32 lists three additional filing rules of which you should be aware. Read them.

Three Additional Rules

Answer 26
St. Joan of Arc. *The SAI of* Saint *comes before SAN of* San Louis.

Answer 27
Tray a.

The following rules are used by most libraries in filing cards in the card catalog:

1. Cards are arranged alphabetically by the first word on the card, ignoring initial articles *a*, *an*, and *the*. If the article appears in the body of the title, it is considered in filing.

2. Cards are filed word by word rather than letter by letter.

Word by Word	Letter by Letter
New Jersey	Newark
New York	New Jersey
Newark	Newspapers
Newspapers	New York

3. Names beginning with *Mc*, *M'*, and *Mac* are filed as if spelled MAC.

4. Numbers are filed as if spelled out. For example, 103 becomes "one hundred and three."

5. Abbreviations are filed as though spelled out:

   Mr. = Mister
   Dr. = Doctor
   St. = Saint
   however
   Mrs. = Mrs.
   (This is an exception to the rule.)

6. On words ending in *'s*, the apostrophe is dropped and the *s* is considered part of the word in filing.

7. Compound surnames are filed immediately after the simple surname and before subject and title headings.

8. For a surname such as *Glass*, all author cards are filed before title and subject heading cards with the same name.

FIG. 1

FIG. 2

SECTION 2 PROGRAM CALL NUMBERS

Section 2 of the Library Card Catalog Workbook deals with the use of call numbers. We see illustrated in figure 1 a "call number" that is not a library call number, but it is not too far off.

Every book in the library has a call number. From your past visits to the library you are probably aware that a book's call number is an identification number that indicates the book's subject, author, and location in the library. The filing system itself is called the *Dewey Decimal* system. When a book comes to the library, it is assigned a call number according to the subject and author; it is then placed on a shelf in the appropriate location with other books with generally similar call numbers. Author, title, and subject cards are filled out for the book and filed in the card catalog. A person then has only to look up the card to find the call number and thus the location of a book.

It's easy to find the call number on the catalog card because it always appears in the same place.

Call Number

Question 1
Look at figure 2. In which corner of the card is the call number found?

The call number is always found in the upper left-hand corner. It may appear elsewhere on the card for the librarians' use, but you need not concern yourself with these references. Also, as you will note in figure 2 again, there are several numbers and letters associated with and below the call number. Some of these markings are important to you and are referred to later in the workbook.

Sample Call Number Chart

Call Number	Level	Call Number	Level	Call Number	Level
000-049	5	160-199	4	600-649	2
050-079	1	200-299	4	650-659	1
080-099	5	M200-M299	4	660-699	2
100-129	4	300-399	1	700-799	5
130-139	1	400-499	5	800-899	5
140-149	4	500-599	2	900-999	4
150-159	1				

Symbol	Location
Americana	Rm. 407 - Special Collections
Arabic	4th Level - Stacks
Asian Collection	4th Level - Stacks
Braille	Rm. 407 - Special Collections
Burns	Rm. 407 - Special Collections
Canadian Document	2nd Level - Documents Collection
Clark	Rm. 407 - Special Collections
Cur E	1st Level - Curriculum Collection
Cur S	1st Level - Curriculum Collection
Curriculum Ref.	1st Level - Curriculum Collection
Documents Collection	2nd Level
File	Rm. 407 - Special Collections
Film	Rm. 426 - Microfilm Rm.
Filmstrip	5th Level - Desk
Grant	Rm. 407 - Special Collections
H080	Rm. 407 - Special Collections
Hafen	Rm. 407 - Special Collections
IRC	Rm. 407 - Special Collections
L. C.	Rm. 407 - Pioneer Rm.
M200-M299	4th Level
Map Collection	2nd Level
Melville	Rm. 407 - Special Collections
Microcard	Rm. 426 - Microfilm Rm.
Microfiche	Rm. 426 - Microfilm Rm.
Microprint	Rm. 426 - Microfilm Rm.
Music	5th Level
Music Research	5th Level
Phonodisc	5th Level - Listening Library
Presses	Rm. 407 - Special Collections
Rare	Rm. 407 - Special Collections
Ref.	3rd Level
Ref. 1	1st Level
Ref. 4	4th Level
Ref. 5	5th Level
Rowe	Rm. 407 - Special Collections
Sci. Ref.	2nd Level
Vault	Rm. 407 - Special Collections
Victorian	Rm. 407 - Special Collections
Welsh	4th Level - Stacks
Whitman	Rm. 407 - Special Collections

The symbols *OS, f, q* above or before the call number indicate oversized books shelved at the end of each major call number section.

FIG. 3

Answer 1
The **upper left-hand corner** *is correct.*

Once you know the call number for a book, it is important that you know where to locate the book in the library. Usually, there are call number charts located near the card catalog in the library. These charts should direct you to the area that houses the particular call number and book for which you are looking. These charts may look similar to the one in figure 3.

Question 2
Look at the chart in figure 3 and decide on which level you would find a book with the call number 520.

Question 3
Look at figure 4. On which level in the library would this book be located according to the chart in figure 3?

Question 4
On which level would the book indicated in figure 5 be located according to the chart in figure 3?

Question 5
If the book in figure 5 had been numbered 653, on which level would it have been found?

```
435
M85        Moser, Virgil, 1882-
G              Frühneuhochdeutsche grammatik, von Virgil Moser ...
           Heidelberg, C. Winter, 1929-

               v. 20 cm. (Added t.-p.: Germanische bibliothek ... I. Sammlung
           germanischer elementar und handbücher. I. reihe: Grammatiken. 17.
           bd.

               "Literaturverzeichnis": v. 1, p. xviii-xliii.


               1. German language—Early modern (to 1700)—Grammar. I. Title.

                                                                    35-18346

           Library of Congress            PF4521.M6
                                                                         435
                                    [2]
```

FIG. 4

```
629.40148
M853s     Moser, Reta C
               Space-age acronyms: abbreviations and designations, by
           Reta C. Moser. With a foreword by Bill M. Woods. New York,
           Plenum Press, 1964.

               427 p. 26 cm.



               1. Astronautics—Abbreviations. 2. Aeronautics—Abbreviations. 3.
           Acronyms. I. Title.

           TL788.M6               629.40148                  64-20744

           Library of Congress           [7-1]
```

FIG. 5

```
Clark
320.53
Al        The Moscow trial. Authentic report: The indictment. Pro-
#749      ceedings. Prosecutor's speech. Defence. The verdict. The
          red paper (litvinov). New York City, Worker's library pub-
          lishers [n.d.] 63p.




              1. Trials - Russia. 2. Moscow - History - 1917-1921.
```

FIG. 6

Remember: Your first concern in using the call number is to locate the area in the library in which a particular book is found. The first few digits give that information. Once you have arrived at that general area, the remaining digits and letters in the call number help you find the book on the shelf.

There is, however, an exception to the above stated rule. Look at figure 6. There is something different about this call number. It is the word *Clark* found as part of the call number. Looking again at the call number chart in figure 3, you will notice that on the left half of the chart, a little way down the column, is the word *Clark*.

Special Location Designations

Question 6
What is the location given on the chart in figure 3 for the "Clark" collection?

_____

You will notice that an entire section of the call number chart is devoted to special locations in the library. Many of the cards you look up in the card catalog will have a special reference, such as Clark, Hafen, Ref. 1, and so forth, included with the call number. These notations indicate special book collections and locations in the library, and you should disregard the call number itself in finding the appropriate area, referring to the *special location* indicated in the call number chart instead.

```
L.C.
808.831      Lockridge, Frances Louise (Davis)
L8131


             The  long  skeleton  [by]  Frances  and  Richard
             Lockridge. New York, Pyramid books [1963 c 1958]
                160p. (Greendoor mystery)




             I. Lockridge, Richard, 1898- jt. au. II. Title.
```

FIG. 7

```
Ref.
015.47       Moscow. Lenin Library.
M851s
             Svodny  katalog  russkoi  knygy,  grazhdanskoia  pechati
             XVIII veka, 1725-1800. Moscow, 196-

                v. facsims.




             1. Russian literature - 18th cent. - Bibl.
```

FIG. 8

Question 7
Look at figure 7. The special notation here is L.C. Where would this book be found in the library according to the call number chart in figure 3?

_____

Question 8
If you mistakenly overlooked the L.C. notation for the book in figure 7, where would you look for this book without success?

_____

Question 9
Figure 8 again shows the importance of noting the correct location. Give the location of this book according to the call number chart in figure 3.

_____

Question 10
Where might you mistakenly have looked for the book in figure 8 if you had not been careful in noting the call number?

_____

If you are not familiar with some of the areas referred to on the call number chart in your library, we would suggest that you check with the general reference librarian for special orientation and directions.

Answer 7
Room 407 *is the correct answer, according to the sample call number chart.*

Answer 8
Level 5 — *without success.*

Answer 9
Level 3.

Answer 10
Level 5.

Every book in the library has a call number—an I.D. number which indicates where in the library it is located. As can be seen on the card below, the call number is located in the upper left-hand corner of the card. It always appears there.

Call number charts direct you to the proper area of the library once you know the call number. Such charts are located near the card catalog in most libraries.

Some cards in the card catalog will have a special notation in the call number, such as "Clark," or "Americana." Such notations indicate special collections in the library and these books will be found in special locations. Again, refer to the call number chart for the exact area.

823
B31c   Catherine Foster.

Bates, Herbert Ernest, 1905-

Catherine Foster. London. Jonathan Cape. [1929]
256p.

I. Title.

Canopus, Decree of.

See

Decree of Canopus.

FIG. 1

SECTION 3 PROGRAM CROSS-REFERENCE CARDS

Most of the cards in the card catalog are either author, title, or subject cards. They each contain much important information, including the book's call number, author, and title and a brief description of its contents. These three kinds of cards look very much alike. However, there is one type of card in the card catalog that does not resemble the author, title, or subject cards at all. It is a cross-reference card, often referred to as a "see" or "see also" card. Figure 1 shows an example of a "see" card.

Question 1
What purpose do you think the card in figure 1 serves?

_____

_____

_____

_____

The "see" card tells us essentially that if you are looking for "Canopus, Decree of," you will find it filed under *Decree of Canopus*. The "see" card is found *in place of* what you are looking for, telling you where to go to find it. Such a card is also used for an author who writes under a pseudonym (a false name).

"See" Card

Answer 1
Your answer should be: **It tells you that you are looking under the wrong heading and refers you to the correct one.**

Canot, Theodore [pseud.]

See

Conneau, Théophile

FIG. 2

Canning and preserving

See also

Borax

also subdivision Preservation under names of individual foods, e.g. Fishery products - Preservation.

FIG. 3

Calculus of tensors

See also

Spaces, Generalized
Spinor analysis

FIG. 4

Question 2
Look at figure 2. Under what name would you find a card for this author?

_____

"See Also" Card

The "see also" cross-reference card is similar to the "see" card; however, instead of being a substitute for the card you are looking for, it tells you where to go for *additional* information. Figure 3 illustrates a "see also" card.

If you were to look up the subject *canning and preserving,* you would probably find several subject cards in the card catalog under that subject heading. At the end of those cards you would find the "see also" card referring you to still other related subject headings.

Question 3
What is the other subject heading related to canning and preserving on the card in figure 3 which it suggests you might look up?

_____

Question 4
Look at figure 4. What other two subject headings are you referred to?

_____

_____

Remember: the "see card" is found in place of what you are looking for. The "see also" card is found in addition to what you have already found.

Question 5
Where is a "see also" card found in relation to the other cards with the same subject heading — before or after?

_____

Remember, also: subject headings are always found in *red;* these are not book titles. Section 4 goes into detail about subject headings and subject cards.

Answer 2
Conneau, Theophile *is correct.* Canot, Theodore *is a pseudonym.*

Answer 3
Borax. *It also suggests that you could look under individual foods, such as* fishery products, *and then subdivisions such as* preservation.

Answer 4
Spaces, Generalized *and* **Spinor analysis** *are the other two subject headings.*

Answer 5
The "see also" card comes **after** *all the others with the same subject heading.*

One kind of card in the card catalog is called the cross-reference card. It is sometimes referred to as the ''see'' or ''see also'' card. Two examples of such cards are shown below.

Canopus, Decree of.

See

Decree of Canopus.

Canning and preserving

See also

Borax

   also subdivision Preservation under names of individual foods, e.g. Fishery products - Preservation.

As can be seen by the above examples, such cards (1) point you in the right direction when you are looking under an incorrect name or heading or (2) give you additional subject heading suggestions to which you might refer.

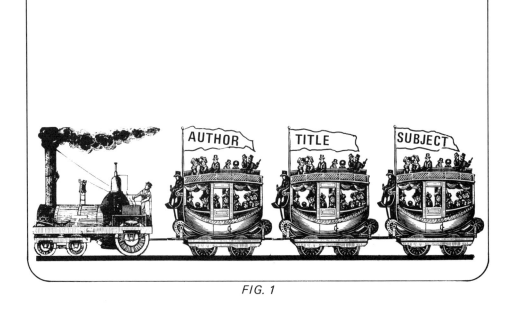

FIG. 1

SECTION 4 PROGRAM AUTHOR, TITLE, AND SUBJECT CARDS

Four Kinds of Cards

There are primarily four kinds of cards in the card catalog: author, title, subject, and cross-reference cards. Section 3 dealt with cross-reference cards, instructing us that these are important aids in the library. However, the author, title, and subject cards are the ones which actually describe the books in the library collection.

As illustrated in figure 1, author, title, and subject cards may seem quite similar to each other in appearance. They each contain the author's name, the book title, and other descriptive information about the book. You might ask, then, why does the card catalog include the three different kinds of cards if each has the same information? The answer is, of course, to help you find the book you are looking for more easily, whether you have complete or only partially complete reference information.

Though it is not always the case, there are normally three cards in the card catalog for every book in the library — each filed alphabetically. That would mean you could find a book by looking up the author's name, the book title, or the subject of the book.

201
L25   Lang, G   H

    The modern gift of tongues: whence is it? A testimony and an examination. London, New York, Marshall Brothers, [n.d.]
      132 p.

    1. Glossolalia. I. Title.

a

201
L25   The modern gift of tongues.

      Lang, G   H

    The modern gift of tongues: whence is it? A testimony and an examination. London, New York, Marshall Brothers, [n.d.]
      132 p.

    1. Glossolalia. I. Title.

b

      Glossolalia.
201
L25

      Lang, G   H
    The modern gift of tongues: whence is it? A testimony and an examination. London, New York, Marshall Brothers, [n.d.]
      132 p.

    1. Glossolalia. I. Title.

c

FIG. 2

Question 1
Look at the three cards illustrated in figure 2. These are an author card, a title card, and a subject card for the book *The Modern Gift of Tongues.* *Is the first line on card* a *in figure 2 an author, title, of subject heading?*

_____

Question 2
Is card a *of figure 2 an author, title, or subject card?*

_____

Question 3
Look at card b *in figure 2. The first line of this card is the title* The Modern Gift of Tongues. *Card* b *is what kind of card?*

_____

Question 4
Card c *in figure 2 is a subject card. What easily noticed characteristic of the subject card makes it readily distinguishable from author and title cards?*

_____

Answer 1
The author's name, Lang.

Answer 2
An author card.

Answer 3
A title card.

Answer 4
The subject heading appears in red print.

Peddlers and peddling - U.S.

658.85
G565f   Golden, Harry Lewis, 1902-
            Forgotten pioneer. Illustrated by Leonard Vosburgh. [1st ed.] Cleveland, World Pub. Co. [1963]

            157 p. illus. 21 cm.

            Includes bibliography.

            1. Peddlers and peddling—U.S. 2. Jews in the U.S. I. Title.

            HF5459.U6G6   658.8554   63—11958

            Library of Congress   [63g10]

380.9737
D685y   Peddlers and peddling — U.S.

            Dolan, J   R

            The yankee peddlers of early America, by J. R. Dolan. [1st ed.] New York, C. N. Potter [1964]
            270 p. illus. 25 cm.

            Bibliography: p. 267-270.

            1. Peddlers and peddling—U.S. 2. U.S.—Soc. life & cust.—Colonial period. 3. U.S.—Soc. life & cust.   1. Title.

            HF5459.U6D6   380.973   63-19902

            Library of Congress   [6519]

FIG. 3

                    Philosophy of recent times.
190
H255p   Hartman, James B   *comp.*
                Philosophy of recent times, edited by James B. Hartman. New York, McGraw-Hill [1966-67]

main body   2 v. 24 cm.

                Includes bibliographies.

                CONTENTS.—v. 1. Readings in nineteenth-century philosophy.—v. 2. Readings in twentieth-century philosophy.

                1. Philosophy, Modern—19th cent. 2. Philosophy—Collections. I. Title.
                B803.H324   190   66-25478 rev
                Library of Congress   [r67i5]

FIG. 4

The subject heading on subject cards always appears in red print at the top of the card.

Question 5
Could you have more than one card in the card catalog with the same subject heading?

There may be many cards which have the same subject heading, but each would have a different title. For example, look at figure 3.

Question 6
Figure 3 illustrates two cards which have the same subject heading. Do they have the same title?

Question 7
Write the title of each book in figure 3.

On most cards in the card catalog, there is a simple way of finding the title, author, and subject heading. Look at figure 4. Note the information on the card which has been designated as the "main body."

Question 8
What is the first information that appears in the main body — an author, subject heading, or title?

The title of the book is the first information to appear in the main body of the information on the card.

Answer 5
Certainly.

Answer 6
No, *they don't.*

Answer 7
Forgotten Pioneer *and* **The Yankee Peddlers of Early America** *are the titles of the two books.*

Answer 8
The book **title.** *In this case the title is* **Philosophy of Recent Times.**

Poets, American.

821.9109
B75   Brenner, Rica.
               Poets of our time, by Rica Brenner ... New York, Harcourt, Brace and company [ᶜ1941]

               xii, 411 p. ports. 21 ᶜᵐ.

               CONTENTS.—Stephen Vincent Benét.—Archibald MacLeish.—Vachel Lindsay.—Thomas Stearns Eliot.—Sara Teasdale.—Wystan Hugh Auden.—Stephen Spender.—Elinor Wylie.—William Butler Yeats.

               1. American poetry—20th cent.—Hist. & crit. 2. English poetry—20th cent.—Hist. & crit. 3. Poets, American. 4. Poets, English. I. Title.

                                                                        41-51653
       Library of Congress   PR603.B68

               Copy 2.   [18]   821.9109

FIG. 5

Question 9
What information appears directly above the title on the card in figure 4?

_____

The example illustrated in figure 4 shows the usual relationship between the title and the author listing on the card, should a particular listing confuse you.

Question 10
In the example in figure 4, there is something listed at the top of the card above the author's name. What is it?

_____

Question 11
What kind of card, then, is the card in figure 4?

_____

Question 12
Look at figure 5. What is listed at the top of this card?

_____

Question 13
What kind of card, then, is the card in figure 5?

_____

Remember: a card is filed alphabetically in the card catalog according to the first word on the card, whether it is a title, an author's name, or a subject heading (unless the first word is an article — *a*, *an*, or *the*).

First Word Filing

Answer 9
The **author's name**, *James B.*
Hartman.

Answer 10
Again it is the **title** —
Philosophy of Recent Times.

Answer 11
The correct answer is a **title**
card.

Answer 12
The **subject heading** — *Poets,*
American.

Answer 13
It is, of course, a **subject card**.

Perry, George Sessions, 1910-1956.

810.9
So89   Alexander, Stanley Gerald.
#13   George Sessions Perry, by Stanley G. Alexander. Austin,
            Tex., Steck-Vaughn Co. [1967]

                II, 44 p. 21 cm. (Southwest writers series, no. 18)

                Bibliography: p. 37-44.

                1. Perry, George Sessions, 1910-1956.   (Series)

                PS3531.E687Z56   818'.5208   67-25231

            Library of Congress   [3]

FIG. 6

Question 14
The subject heading Poets,
American *would be filed
under what word?*

_____

Question 15
*Figure 6 illustrates an ex-
ample of a card which might
be confusing. Who is the
author?*

_____

Question 16
*Which two entries are the
same on the card in figure 6?*

_____

_____

Remember: a person can be the subject of a book if it is *about* him.
Sometimes the title and the subject heading may even be the same — as is the
case in figure 6. Find the main body of the card and work backward from
there, you should have no problem identifying title, author, and subject
heading.

The books *about* an author are always filed in the card catalog *after* books
by that same author. This is an important rule for you to remember. For
example, if you want to find something about Shakespeare in the library,
don't make the mistake of looking through all the cards in the catalog for
books written by Shakespeare. Go directly to the end of those cards *by* him,
and there you will find the books *about* him.

By before **About**

Answer 14
Poets.

Answer 15
In this case, **Stanley Gerald Alexander.** *If you find the main body first, then the title, the first thing above the title is the author's name.*

Answer 16
The **subject heading** *and the* **title** *are both the same.*

a

Mor
M288.1
D334f   Day, Willard A

Forty three poems. Salt Lake City, Ray Printing Co., c1958.
51p.

On cover: Crude oil; mental lubrication.

1. Mormons - Poetry. I. Title. II. Title: Crude oil.

b

362.71   Day nurseries.
B39w

Beer, Ethel S
Working mothers and the day nursery. New York, Whiteside and Morrow, 1957.

189 p. 21 cm.

1. Day nurseries.   I. Title.

HV851.B42   362.71   57-9698

Library of Congress   [58k10]

FIG. 7

Remember: all the books an author has written will be filed before books others have written about him. This same relationship carries over to other problems like the following. Look at figure 7. It illustrates a subject card and an author card beginning with the same word — *Day*. The author's name is *Day, Willard A.* and the subject heading is *Day Nurseries*.

Remember: subject cards, with red headings, generally come at the end of any given section.

Subject Cards Last

Answer 17
The cards about *Shakespeare*
will all have Shakespeare,
William *in red print at the*
top.

Answer 18
Card a *is the correct answer.*

In the card catalog you will find author, title, and subject cards. Author cards have the author's last name first and are filed in the card catalog under that name. On a title card, the book title appears first and the card is filed under that title. On a subject card, the subject of the book appears on the top of the card in red print, as in the card below.

```
                    Poets, American.
821.9109
B75      Brenner, Rica.
             Poets of our time, by Rica Brenner ... New York, Har-
         court, Brace and company [ᶜ1941]

             xii, 411 p. ports. 21 ᶜᵐ.

             CONTENTS.—Stephen  Vincent  Benét.—Archibald  MacLeish.—
         Vachel Lindsay.—Thomas Stearns Eliot.—Sara Teasdale.—Wystan Hugh
         Auden.—Stephen Spender.—Elinor Wylie.—William Butler Yeats.

             1. American poetry—20th cent.—Hist. & crit. 2. English poetry-
         —20th cent.—Hist. & crit. 3. Poets, American. 4. Poets, English. I. Title.

                                                          41-51653
             Library of Congress          PR603.B68

                 Copy 2.            [18]                 821.9109
```

There may be only one or there may be many cards under a particular subject heading. If there are many, you would know many books have been written on this particular subject.

A person's name may be the subject of a book (and consequently appear in red print at the top) if that person is the subject of the book.

A book title and subject heading may be the same should such a coincidence arise.

Books **about** an author are filed after books **by** the same author.

Cards with the same subject heading are filed by author's last name, and any title cards by the same name as the subject heading are filed within the subject cards—also by author's last name.

Below is a sample library card on which the author, title, and publication information have been indicated. As you will note, the title is the first thing in the "main body" of the card; the publication information follows shortly thereafter. The author's name appears directly above the title. It is usually in darker print and offset a little to the left.

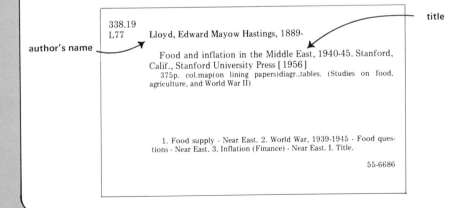

```
                                                              title
338.19
L77      Lloyd, Edward Mayow Hastings, 1889-

             Food and inflation in the Middle East, 1940-45. Stanford,
         Calif., Stanford University Press [1956]
             375p. col.map(on  lining  papers)diagr.,tables. (Studies on food,
         agriculture, and World War II)



             1. Food supply · Near East. 2. World War, 1939-1945 · Food ques-
         tions · Near East. 3. Inflation (Finance) · Near East. I. Title.

             55-6686
```

author's name

251.08
M853p   Moser-Rath, Elfriede, *ed.*
             Predigtmärlein der Barockzeit; ... ..., .vank
         und Fabel in geistlichen Quellen de ... ... mt
         Berlin, De Gruyter, 1964.

             xvi, 511 p. 25 cm. (Supplement Se ...
         Erzahlforschung. Reihe A, Texte, Bd. 5 ...

             Bibliography: p. [511 ...

             1. Sermons, German—Hist. ... crit. 2. Catholic ... Sermons—
         Hist. & crit. 3. Homiletical illustr ... Hist. & crit. ... le. (Series:
         Fabula. Supplement Serie. Reih ... Bd. 5)

         BV4208.G3M6   64-57943
         Library of Congress   [1]

FIG. 1

338.19
L77   Lloyd, Edward Mayow Hastings, 1889-

             Food and inflation in the Middle East, 1940-45. Stanford,
         Calif., Stanford University Press [1956]
             375p. col.map(on lining papers)diagr.,tables. (Studies on food,
         agriculture, and World War II)

tracings

             1. Food supply - Near East. 2. World War, 1939-1945 - Food ques-
         tions - Near East. 3. Inflation (Finance) - Near East. I. Title.

                                                               55-6686

FIG. 2

SECTION 5 PROGRAM TRACINGS

Section 5 of the Library Card Catalog Workbook deals with the "tracings" on the library catalog cards. Author, title, and subject cards all contain special information which librarians call "tracings." Our sleuth in figure 1 is not completely off base in illustrating what these tracings are. Actually, they are very valuable in research. To see how they are used, refer to figure 2.

In figure 2 the tracings have been illustrated on a sample catalog card. As you can see, the tracings are easy to locate and identify. They always appear toward the bottom of the card and are distinguished from the other information on the card by their numbers. You will notice both arabic and roman numerals are used with the tracings. The arabic numerals appear first in the tracings. We will discuss them in detail in a moment.

The roman numerals are for the librarians' reference and simply indicate title and added entry cards that are available for this particular book. For the card in figure 2, the roman numeral I in the tracings tells us that we could find on file in the card catalog a title card for this particular book, in addition to the author card we are looking at in figure 2.

Arabic Numerals

Now, direct your attention to the information numbered with arabic numerals in figure 2. The indicated book is entitled *Food and Inflation in the Middle East*. Each arabic-numbered item in the tracings refers to a subject heading which you could look up in the card catalog to find information related to this particular book.

For the card in figure 2, there are three subject headings listed to which tracings refer you. The first is "Food Supply — Near East." The second is "World War 1939-1945 — Food Question — Near East."

FIG. 3

Question 1
What is the third heading
listed in the tracings in figure
2?

_____

_____

All three subject headings listed in the tracings in figure 2 are related to this particular book, *Food and Inflation in the Middle East.* Should you decide to look them up in the course of your research, you would find them as subject headings in red print in the proper alphabetical locations in the card catalog.

Now, refer to the card illustrated in figure 3. The title of this book is *Microeconomic Analysis.* Find the tracings on the card. Remember that the tracings are separated from the main body of the card and are found near the bottom.

**Gives Additional
Subject Headings**

Question 2
How many subject headings
do the tracings on the card in
figure 3 refer you to?

_____

Question 3
Write the two subject headings referred to in the tracings
in figure 3.

_____

_____

Remember: the roman numeral does not indicate a subject heading. It is for the librarians' use. At this point, it may be helpful to note that only two to four of the major subjects treated in a given book are listed in the tracings. Though the tracings may be helpful, they are not a complete list of the book's contents.

251.08
M853p   Moser-Rath, Elfriede, *ed.*
          Predigtmärlein der Barockzeit; Exempel, Sage, Schwank und Fabel in geistlichen Quellen des oberdeutschen Raumes. Berlin, De Gruyter, 1964.

          xvi, 544 p. 25 cm. (Supplement-Serie zu Fabula; Zeitschrift für Erzählforschung. Reihe A: Texte, Bd. 5)

          Bibliography: p. [514]-533.

          1. Sermons, German—Hist. & crit. 2. Catholic Church—Sermons—Hist. & crit. 3. Homiletical illustrations—Hist. & crit.   I. Title. (Series: Fabula. Supplement Serie. Reihe A: Texte, Bd. 5)

BV4208.G3M6   64-57943

Library of Congress   [1]

FIG. 4

Local church councils.

280.1
Sa56c   Sanderson, Ross Warren, 1884-
          Church cooperation in the United States; the nation-wide backgrounds and ecumenical significance of state and local councils of churches in their historical perspective. [New York] Association of Council Secretaries, 1960.

          272 p. 25 cm.

          Includes bibliography.

          1. Local church councils. 2. Interdenominational cooperation. 3. Christian union—Hist. I. Title.

BV626.S3   280.1   60—13189

Library of Congress   [61f3]

FIG. 5

Question 4
Look at figure 4 and decide how many subject headings are suggested by the tracings.

_____

Let us now see how the tracings could be of help to you in a research project. Suppose you wanted to do a paper on the subject "Local Church Councils." You would first look up that heading in the card catalog and you might find only one card — indicating only one book on this subject. The card you would find is illustrated in figure 5. The title of the book listed on the card is *Church Cooperation in the United States.* If you didn't know how to use the tracings, you would be limited to this one book to use in your research.

Question 5
With your knowledge of tracings, the listing on the card in figure 5 refers you to how many other subject headings?

_____

If you were to look up the other two subject headings in the card catalog, you might find that "interdenominational cooperation" has six books under its heading and that "Christian union history" has an additional eleven books under its heading. This would make a total of seventeen books from which you could choose to do research.

799.297
Sh43w   Sheldon, Charles, 1867-1928.

    The wilderness of Denali; explorations of a hunter-naturalist in northern Alaska, by Charles Sheldon, with an introduction by C. Hart Merriam ... New York, London, C. Scribner's sons, 1930.

    xxv, 412 p. front., plates, ports., fold. map. 24^{cm}.

    Edited by C. H. Merriam and E. W. Nelson. *cf.* Pref.

    1. Hunting—Alaska. 2. McKinley, Mount. 3. Mountain sheep. I. Merriam, Clinton Hart, 1855-1942, ed. II. Nelson, Edward William, 1855-joint ed. III. Title.

                        30—10238

    Library of Congress   SK49.S58

                [a44o1]   [508.798] 799.29798

a

799.297
Sh43wi   Sheldon, Charles, 1867-1928.

    The wilderness of the North Pacific coast islands; a hunter's experiences while searching for wapiti, bears, and caribou on the larger coast islands of British Columbia and Alaska, by Charles Sheldon ... New York, C. Scribner's sons, 1912.

    xvii, 246 p. front., plates, maps (1 fold.) 21½^{cm}.

    CONTENTS.—Hunting the wapiti on Vancouver island, 1904.—Hunting the big bear on Montague island, 1905.—The elusive caribou of the Queen Charlotte islands, 1906.—A woman's experience among the bears of Admiralty island, 1909.—Appendices: A. *Ursus sheldoni,* a new bear from Montague island, Alaska. B. Notes on some habits of the Montague island bear. C. The Queen Charlotte island caribou, *Rangifer dawsoni.*—Index.

    1. Hunting—British Columbia. 2. Hunting—Alaska. I. Title.

                        12—22150

    Library of Congress   SK49.S6

            [42j1]

b

917.121
Sh43   Sheldon, Charles, 1867-1928.   For location of additional copies see next card.

    The wilderness of the upper Yukon; a hunter's explorations for wild sheep in subarctic mountains by Charles Sheldon ... New York, C. Scribner's Sons, 1911.

    xxi, 354p. col. front., plates (part col.) maps (1 fold.)

    List of books relating to sport, natural history and explorations of the Yukon Territory; p. 331-332.

    1. Hunting - Yukon Territory. 2. Yukon Territory - Desc. & trav. 3. Mountain sheep. I. Title.

                        11-25122

c

FIG. 6

The tracings have one other important function that can help you. By telling you which additional subject headings you can refer to, the tracings have indirectly told you what subjects are referred to in a particular book itself. Let us see an example of how this can be helpful. Suppose you know that Charles Sheldon has written a book which contains specific references in it to "mountain sheep." You don't want to read the three books he has written to find which one has what you want, and it would waste time to look up the three books and read their summaries. However, the tracings on each of the cards can often help you.

Question 6
Look at the sample cards in figure 6. All three are books by Charles Sheldon. Two of the cards make reference to mountain sheep in their tracings. One does not. Which one is it, a,b, *or* c?

Note that this does not necessarily say that the book in card *b does not* deal with mountain sheep. It might. But it is probably not a major topic of the book since no mention of it is made in the tracings; and you may save time by leaving this particular book until last as you search for information.

Answer 6
The correct answer is **b.**

Author, title, and subject cards in the card catalog contain special information the librarians call "tracings." The tracings have been indicated on the card below.

```
133.82
R792c      Flying saucers

           Rowe, Kelvin, 1908-

               A call at dawn; a message from our brothers of the
           planets Pluto and Jupiter.
           Illustrations by M. Swift.      El Monte, Calif., Understanding
           Publishing Co. [c1955]
               198p. illus.



tracings ──────▶

               1. Thought-transference.   2. Flying saucers. I. Title.
```

The roman numerals on the card are for the librarians' use. They indicate other title and added entry cards filed on this book. The arabic numerals are valuable tools in using the card catalog effectively. They serve two main purposes: (1) they direct you to additional subject headings to which you could refer and (2) they give you some of the main subjects treated in the book.

For the card above, the tracings tell you that (1) you could look up the subject headings "Thought transference" and "Flying Saucers" for more and related books and (2) this particular book, *A Call at Dawn*, deals with "thought transference" and "flying saucers."

Dairy Chemistry

see

Dairy products
Analysis and Examination

FIG. 1

6

PROGRAM

SUBJECT HEADINGS IN THE LIBRARY OF CONGRESS

"SHLC"

One important tool to aid you in using the card catalog is the book entitled *Subject Headings Used in the Dictionary Catalogs of the Library of Congress* (SHLC). It is a large book resembling an unabridged dictionary in size. You should check at the general reference desk or with the general reference librarian for its exact location in the library.

There are several ways this book can be important to you when you are using the card catalog. For instance, it is nearly impossible for a library to list every card under every possible subject heading. As you are aware, librarians file in appropriate places "see" and "see also" cards, referring you to the correct place in the card catalog to find your information. The librarian uses SHLC to obtain that *correct* subject heading to refer you to. However, most libraries do not have "see" and "see also" cards for every heading listed in SHLC. If you were looking for a particular subject heading in the card catalog and could not find a card for it, your next step should be to look up that heading in SHLC. It would tell you what subject heading to look under to find your information.

Alternate Subject Headings

Suppose you wanted to find the subject heading *dairy chemistry* and found no such heading in the card catalog. Your next step should be to look up that heading alphabetically in SHLC. Figure 1 illustrates what you might find.

Question 1
From the illustration in figure 1, what subject heading would you look under in the card catalog to find information on dairy chemistry?

_____

_____

Proteinase, Alkali

see

Trypsin

FIG. 2

Answer 1

*Figure 1 tells you to "*see **Dairy Products — analysis and examination.**" *This is the same suggestion you would be given by a "see" card filed in the card catalog.*

Question 2
Suppose you had looked up the subject proteinase alkali *in the card catalog and had found nothing. You would next go to SHLC, where you would find that heading listed alphabetically. Figure 2 illustrates what you might see. What does it tell you about where to look in the card catalog?*

Related Subject Headings

The book SHLC has other uses than just directing you to a heading not filed in the card catalog. Let us suppose you wanted to do some research on the subject *family*. There would be many ways you could go about finding information on the subject. The most obvious would be to start looking for cards in the card catalog under that particular subject heading. From there you could refer to the tracings on the cards you found and, by looking up those related headings, you could find a great deal of information to help you. However, let us suggest an alternative using SHLC that many times will be of help to you.

Question 3
How many subject headings can you think of which are related to the subject family *which you could find in the card catalog? List all the subjects you can think of, such as* parents, children, *or* finances.

_____

_____

_____

_____

_____

_____

Each such subject heading listed in SHLC would be a source for several books related to *family*, and these books in turn would be potential sources of information for your research.

Answer 2

It would tell you to look in the card catalog under **trypsin**.

Answer 3

There are some **forty** possible related subject headings to which you could refer for help. The book lists all of them, and each subject heading would be a source of several books related to family.

Fairs (Continued)
   Manners and customs
   Markets
   —Juvenile literature
Fairy plays (Juvenile, PN6120.A4-5)
   x Plays, Fairy
Fairy poetry (PN6110.F3)
   xx Fairies
   Fairy tales
   Poetry
Fairy tales (Folk-lore, GR550; History and criticism, PN3437; Juvenile works, PZ8, PZ14, PZ24; Occultism, BF1552)
   sa Folk-lore
   xx Children's literature
   Children's stories
   Fiction
   Folk-lore
   Legends
   Literature
   —Classification (GR550; Z5983.F17)
      Here are entered lists of fairy tales, or of their types, themes, motives, variants, etc., compiled with the aim of arranging them in certain clearly defined groups, also treatises discussing the principles upon which systems of classification may be based. Whenever desirable, additional entry is made under Folk-lore—Classification.
      sa Literature, Comparative—Themes, motives
      Plots (Drama, novel, etc.)
      x Fairy tales—Themes, motives
      Fairy tales—Types
      xx Literature, Comparative—Themes, motives
      Plots (Drama, novel, etc.)
   —Dictionaries (GR550)
   —Illustrations
   —Indexes
   —Moral and religious aspects
   —Themes, motives
      See Fairy tales—Classification
   —Types
      See Fairy tales—Classification
Faith (Moral theology, BV4637; Theology, BT770-772)
   Here are entered works on religious faith and doubt. Works on belief and doubt from the philosophical standpoint are entered under the heading Belief and doubt.
   sa Agnosticism
   Apostasy
   Atheism
   Evidence
   Faith and reason
   Hope
   Rule of faith
   Salvation
   Sanctification
   Skepticism
   Trust in God
   Truth
   x Religious belief
   xx Belief and doubt
   Christian life
   Credulity
   Justification
   Religion
   Spiritual life
   Theological virtues
   Theology, Doctrinal
   Trust in God
   —Early works to 1800
   —Juvenile literature

"see also"

related source

"dashes"

Faith, Confessions of
   See Creeds
Faith, Profession of
   See Profession of faith
Faith, Rule of
   See Rule of faith
Faith and justification
   See Justification
Faith and reason (BT50)
   Here are entered works on the proper limits, differences, similarities, and interaction of the knowledge attained through faith and that attained through reason. Works more general in scope are entered under Philosophy and religion, or Religion and science.
   x Logic and faith
   Reason and faith
   xx Apologetics
   Faith
   Knowledge, Philosophy
   Rationalism
   Reason
   Religion and science
Faith-cure (BT732.5; Medical aspects, RZ400-401)
   sa Christian Science
   Healing gods
   Incubation (in religion, folk-lore, etc.)
   Jewish Science
   Magnetic healing
   Medicine, Magic, mystic, and spagiric
   Mental healing
   Miracles
   Therapeutics, Suggestive
   x Divine healing
   Faith healing
   Mind-cure
   Spiritual healing
   xx Christian Science
   Medicine and religion
   Mental healing
   Mind and body
   Subconsciousness
   Therapeutics, Suggestive
Faith healing
   See Faith-cure
Fakirs (BL2015.F2)
   x Bhikshu
   Faqirs
   xx Asceticism
   Dervishes
   Mohammedanism
   Yoga
Falashas (Ethiopia, DT380; Jews, DS135.E75)
   x Fenjas
   Foggara
   Kaila
   xx Jews
Falcidian law
   See Legitime
Falcon (Missile)
   x Air-to-air missiles
   Anti-aircraft missiles
   Falcon missiles
Falcon missiles
   See Falcon (Missile)
Falconry (Indirect) (SK321)
   sa Fowling
   x Hawking
   xx Fowling
   Game and game-birds
   Hunting
   —Juvenile literature

Falcons (QL696.A2)
   xx Birds of prey
Fali (African people)
   xx Ethnology—Cameroons, French
Falicaine
   xx Anesthetics
Falkland Islands, Battle of the, 1914 (D582.F2)
   xx European War, 1914-1918—Naval operations
Fall
   See Autumn
Fall army-worms (SB945.A8)
   x Grassworm
   xx Army-worms
Fall of man (BT710)
   sa Good and evil
   Paradise
   Sin
   Sin, Original
   x Man, Fall of
   xx Man (Theology)
   Sin
   Sin, Original
   Temptation
   Theology, Doctrinal
   —History of doctrines
Fall River, Mass.
   —Textile Workers' Strike, 1875
      x Fall River Strike, 1875
Fall River Indians
   See Pocasset Indians
Fall River Strike, 1875
   See Fall River, Mass.—Textile Workers' Strike, 1875
Fallacies (Logic) (BC175)
   x Errors, Logical
   Sophistry (Logic)
   xx Judgment (Logic)
   Logic
   Reasoning
Falling-stars
   See Meteors
Fallopian tubes (Comparative anatomy, QL881; Gynecology, RG421-433; Human anatomy, QM421)
   —Radiography
Fallot's tetralogy
   See Tetralogy of Fallot
Fallout, Radioactive
   See Radioactive fallout
Fallout shelters
   See Atomic bomb shelters
Fallow
   See Fallowing
Fallowing
   sa Soil fertility
   x Fallow
   xx Rotation of crops
   Soil fertility
   Tillage
Falls (Accidents) (Direct)
   xx Accidents
   Impact—Physiological effect
Falls Fight, 1676 (E83.67)
   xx King Philip's War, 1675-1676
False brinelling
   See Fretting corrosion
False certification (Direct)
   x Certification, False
   xx Forgery
   Fraud
   Legal documents
   Misconduct in office
False chinch bug
   xx Chinch-bugs

refers back to main heading

FIG. 3

Therapeutics (RM)
   sa Alteratives
   Antipyretics
   Antiseptic medication
   Baunscheidtism
   Bibliotherapy
   Chemistry, Medical and pharmaceutical
   Classification—Books—Therapeutics
   Counter-irritants
   Diaphoresis and diaphoretics
   Diet in disease
   Drugs
   Electrolyte therapy
   Endermic medication
   Homeopathy—Materia medica and therapeutics
   Inhalation therapy
   Injections, Hypodermic
   Intravenous therapy
   Malariotherapy
   Materia medica
   Medicine—Formulae, receipts, prescriptions
   Medicine, Dosimetric
   Medicines, Antagonism of
   Mineral waters
   Narcotics
   Nurses and nursing
   Nutrition
Organotherapy
   Orgonomy
   Parenteral therapy
   Placebo (Medicine)
   Prescription writing
   Purgatives
   Rademacherism
   Rectum, Medication by
   Serumtherapy
   Shock therapy
   Stimulants
   X-rays
   also names of individual drugs, e.g. Belladonna, Strychnine; and names of diseases and groups of diseases, e.g. Bronchitis, Fever, Nervous system—Diseases; and subdivision Therapeutic use under specific subjects, e.g. Alkaloids—Therapeutic use; Poetry—Therapeutic use; X-rays—Therapeutic use
   xx Materia medica
   Medicine—Practice
   Pathology
   —Complications and sequelae (RM103)
   —Early works to 1800 (RM81; RM84)
   —Examinations, questions, etc. (RM126)

FIG. 4

88

Figure 3 illustrates a page from SHLC. Note the *"sa"* notation which has been marked. The *"sa"* means "see also" and is the same as a "see also" card in the card catalog. This *"sa"* notation indicates the *most* related subject headings and consequently the *best* sources for more information. Sometimes there is only one listing by the *"sa,"* and sometimes there are several headings listed.

"sa"

Note the *"xx"* notation in figure 3. An *"xx"* indicates a good heading to look under for additional, though less-related, subject headings.

"xx"

Note the *"x"* notation in figure 3. A single *"x"* is *not* a good heading to look up when you are in search of additional subject headings. It means that if you looked up these headings, you would be referred back to the original heading. For the single *"x"* notation under *Faith and reason* in figure 3, you see *Logic and faith* and *Reason and faith.* If you looked up either of these headings in the card catalog, you would be referred by a "see" card to *Faith and reason.* The *"x"* entries lead to no new subject headings.

"x"

Question 4
Under the main subject heading Faith *in figure 3, how many other related subject headings could you look under, including the "sa" and "xx" headings for more information?*

Look at the bottom of the first column in figure 3 and note the last two headings. They are —*Early Works to 1800* and —*Juvenile Literature.* The dash preceding the headings indicates that these are part of the main heading *Faith.* Thus, you would find the cards for these headings in the card catalog as "Faith — early works to 1800" and "Faith — juvenile literature."

Dash

languages

x Alphabet – Transliteration
  International alphabet
  Transcription (Transliteration)
xx Phonetic alphabet
Transmigration *(Comparative religion, BL525; Philosophy, BD426)*
  sa Pre-existence
    Reincarnation
    Soul
  x Metempsychosis
  xx Animism
    Future life
    Pre-existence
    Reincarnation
    Soul
    Theosophy
Transmission, Power
  See Power transmission
Transmission devices
  See subdivision Transmission devices *under subjects, e.g.* Automobiles – Transmission devices; Tractors – Transmission devices
Transmission of heat
  See Heat – Transmission
Transmission of sound
  See Sound – Transmission
Transmission of texts
  x Literary transmission
    Manuscript transmission
    Textual transmission

Transonic aerodynamics
  See Aerodynamics, Transonic
Transonic speeds
  See Aerodynamics, Transonic
Transonic wind tunnels
  xx Aerodynamics, Transonic
    Wind tunnels
Transparencies *(Photography, TR720-730; Transparency painting, ND1573)*
  sa Lantern slides
  xx Lantern slides
Transpiration (Physics) *(QC185)*
  Transpiration of plants
  See Plants – Transpiration
Transplantation of organs, tissues, etc. *(QP89)*
  sa Cellular therapy
    Immunological tolerance
    Skin-grafting
    Surgery, Plastic
  also subdivision Transplantation *under specific organs, tissues, etc., e.g.* Eye – Transplantation; Cornea – Transplantation; Tissues – Transplantation
  xx Surgery
    Surgery, Experimental
Transplantation of organs, tissues, etc. (Canon law)
  Transplantation of teeth
  See Teeth – Transplantation

Transportation *(Indirect) (HE)*
  sa Acids – Handling and transportation
    Aeronautics, Commercial
    Air travel
    Automobiles
    Bridges
    Cab and omnibus service
    Canals
    Carriages and carts
    Coastwise navigation
    Coastwise shipping
    Commerce
    Communication and traffic
    Commuting
    Delivery of goods
    Electric railroads
    Electricity in transportation
    Express service
    Ferries
    Freight and freightage
    Harbors
    Inland navigation
    Inland water transportation
    Local transit
    Merchant marine
    Ocean travel
    Pack transportation
    Parcels-post
    Pipe lines
    Pneumatic-tube transportation
    Postal service

1316

Railroads
Roads
Route surveying
Shipping
Steam-navigation
Steamboat lines
Storage and moving trade
Street-railroads
Streets
Subways
Trade routes
Traffic engineering
Traffic surveys
Transit, International
Transportation radio stations
Underwater pipe lines
Vehicles
Waterways
  also subdivision Transportation *under special subjects, e.g.* Cattle – Transportation; Farm produce – Transportation; Petroleum – Transportation
  xx Commerce
    Communication and traffic
    Economics
    Locomotion
    Space in economics
    Storage and moving trade
  – Accidents
  – Automation
  – Consolidation
    x Transportation mergers
    Example under Consolidation and merger of corporations
  – Cost of operation
  – Equipment and supplies
  – Fares
    xx Transportation – Rates
  – Finance
    sa Shipping bounties and subsidies
  – Freight
    See Freight and freightage
  – Handbooks, manuals, etc.
    See Shippers' guides
  – Laws and regulations *(HE194-5)*
    sa Carriers
      Highway law
      Interstate commerce
      Maritime law
      Railroad law
    xx Carriers
      Trade regulation
  – Mathematical models
  – Passenger traffic
    sa Segregation in transportation
    x Passenger traffic
  – Passes
    See Passes (Transportation)
  – Pictorial works
  – Production standards
  – Rates *(Railroads, HE1831-2220; Waterways, HE594-601)*
    sa Canals – Rates and tolls
      Railroads – Fares
      Railroads – Rates
      Shipping – Rates
      Shipping conferences
      Transportation – Fares
    x Carriers – Rates
  – Research
  – Safety measures
  – Taxation
    sa Freight and freightage – Taxation
    x Transportation tax

– Time-tables
  x Time-tables (Transportation)
– Vocational guidance *(Engineering, TA1160)*
Transportation, Atomic-powered *(Indirect)*
  sa Atomic aircraft
    Atomic locomotives
    Atomic ships
    Nuclear propulsion
    Nuclear rockets
  x Atomic-powered transportation
    Atomic transportation
    Nuclear transportation
  xx Atomic power
Transportation, Automotive *(Indirect) (HE5601-5720)*
  sa Automobile parking
    Automobiles
    Automobiles – Social aspects
    Automobiles, Company
    Commercial vehicles
    Freight-cars on truck trailers
    Highway transport workers
    Motor bus lines
    Motor buses
    Motor-truck terminals
    Motor-trucks
    Motor vehicles
    Motorization, Military
    School children – Transportation
    Taxicabs
    Traffic police
    Traffic safety
    Traffic surveys
    Truck trailers, Demountable
  x Automotive transportation
    Highway transportation
    Road transportation
  xx Automobiles – Social aspects
  Note under Automobiles – Social aspects
  – Accounting
  – Cases
    x Transportation, Automotive – Laws and regulations – Cases
  – Collective labor agreements
    See Collective labor agreements – Trucking industry
  – Cost of operation
  – Dispatching
  – Employees
    See Highway transport workers
  – Finance
  – Freight
    sa Motor-truck freight
    xx Freight and freightage
  – Freight classification
    sa Transportation, Automotive – Rates
    xx Transportation, Automotive – Rates
  – Laws and regulations *(HE5618.5-5720)*
    sa Carriers
      Traffic regulations
    x Motor carriers
    xx Carriers
    – Cases
      See Transportation, Automotive – Cases
  – Laws and regulations, International
    xx International law
  – Licenses *(Direct)*

1317

– Rates
  sa Transportation, Automotive – Freight classification
  xx Transportation, Automotive – Freight classification
– Records and correspondence
– Taxation *(Direct)*
  sa Motor bus lines – Taxation
  x Motor-trucks – Taxation
  Note under Automobiles – Taxation
– Technological innovations
– Traffic control
  See Traffic signs and signals
Transportation, Military *(UC270-460; Medical service, UH500-505; Naval, VC550-555)*
  sa Airdrop
    Automobiles, Military
    Explosives – Transportation
    Landing craft
    Landing operations
    Military bridges
    Military railroads
    Motorization, Military
    Pack transportation
    Stream crossing, Military
    Trafficability
    Transports
    Vehicles, Military
  also subdivisions Transport of sick and wounded, Transport service *and* Transportation *under armies, e.g.* Germany. Heer – Transport of sick and wounded; Germany. Heer – Transportation; U.S. Army – Transport service
  x Military transportation
    Motor vehicles in war
  xx Communications, Military
    Explosives – Transportation
    Military art and science
    Stream crossing, Military
  – Cold weather conditions
    x Arctic transportation
      Cold weather operations (Military)
    xx Arctic regions
      Ice
      Winter warfare
    Example under reference from Arctic conditions
  – Research *(Direct)*
    xx Military research
Transportation, Primitive *(GN439-440)*
  sa Litters
Transportation insurance
  See Insurance, Inland marine
    Insurance, Marine
Transportation mergers
  See Transportation – Consolidation
Transportation of criminals
  See Penal colonies
Transportation of dangerous goods
  See Dangerous goods, Transportation of
Transportation of merchandise in bond
  See Bonded warehouses and goods
Transportation of prisoners
  See Prisoners, Transportation of
Transportation of school children
  See School children – Transportation
Transportation radio stations *(Direct)*
  xx Radio stations
    Transportation
Transportation tax
  See Transportation – Taxation

dash

FIG. 5

When you are doing your research and make note of the subject headings you want to look up in the card catalog, remember that you are not looking up book titles. You are looking up subject headings, and subject cards are distinguishable by their red print at the top. Once you have looked up the individually related subject headings — each with a number of books on the particular subject — by using the tracings and the book description on the cards, you can most likely come up with considerably more books to use in your research than you could by only looking up the main heading alone. If you so desired, you could continue to use SHLC to find an almost countless number of subject headings related to your subject. In doing this, you would look up individually in SHLC each of the subject headings given, each of which would give you more subject headings. You could in turn look up each of these, and so on. When you found the subject headings you felt would help you the most, you would then go to the card catalog and see what book titles are available under those headings.

> *Question 5*
> *Figure 4 illustrates another sample page from SHLC. How many "sa" subject headings are there under* Therapeutics?

There is another way in which SHLC can be of use to you. Actually, it is the reverse of the suggestion we just finished discussing. With this previous suggestion you learned how you could use SHLC to find many related subject headings and thus expand your research possibilities on any given subject. Now, suppose the subject you want to research is too broad and you must narrow it to a more specific area. Can you see how the book SHLC can help you, especially in showing you what the subareas and related areas to your subject are?

To illustrate, let us suppose you want to do some research in the area of transportation. This is a broad subject, and you may not be aware of all the related subject areas or subareas which you could use for research. Pages 1316 and 1317 of SHLC are illustrated in figure 5.

Any one of the subheadings under *Transportation* in figure 5 might serve you for research purposes instead of the broad heading itself. You might narrow your research to *air travel*, *automobiles*, *bridges*, *canals*, or any of the other headings listed. In addition, there are related areas of transportation such as *atomic powered*, *automotive*, *military*, *primitive*, and so forth, and each has subheadings of its own.

RATO
  See Aeroplanes – Assisted take-off
REAC (Computer)
  See Reac computer
RLF
  See Retrolental fibroplasia
Rabbinical counseling
  See Pastoral counseling (Judaism)
Rabbinical courts *(Direct)*
  x Courts, Rabbinical
    Jews – Courts
  xx Courts, Jewish
Rabbinical literature
  xx Geonic literature
    Hebrew literature
    Jewish literature
    Midrash
    Talmud
Rabbinical seminaries *(Indirect)*
  x Jewish theological seminaries
    Seminaries, Rabbinical
    Theological seminaries, Jewish
  xx Judaism – Study and teaching
Rabbis *(Direct)* *(BM652)*
  sa Amoraim
    Cantors, Jewish
    Chief Rabbinate
    Geonim
    Jews – Biography
    Marbits Torah
    Pastoral counseling (Judaism)
    Pastoral psychology (Judaism)
    Pastoral theology (Judaism)
    Tannaim
  x Jewish rabbis
  xx Jews – Biography
    Judaism – Functionaries
  – Anecdotes, facetiae, satire, etc.
    xx Jews – Anecdotes, facetiae,
      satire, etc.
  – Installation
    See Installation (Rabbis)
  – Ordination
    See Semikhah
Rabbit breeding *(SF453)*
  sa Rabbit breeds
  x Rabbits – Breeding
Rabbit breeds
  sa names of specific breeds, e.g.
    American checkered giant
      rabbits, Chinchilla rabbits
  x Rabbits – Breeds
  xx Rabbit breeding
    Rabbits
Rabbit fur
  xx Fur
Rabbit houses
  See Rabbit hutches
Rabbit hunting
Rabbit hutches
  x Rabbit houses
  xx Rabbits
Rabbits *(Indirect)* *(QL737.R6;
  Breeding, SF451-5; Diseases,
  SF979.R2)*
  sa Cookery (Rabbits)
    Cottontails
    Dutch rabbits
    Hares
    Jack-rabbits
    Rabbit breeds
    Rabbit hutches
  xx Hares
  Example under Game and game-birds
  – Anatomy

  – Breeding
    See Rabbit breeding
  – Breeds
    See Rabbit breeds
  – Diseases *(SF979.R2)*
  – Extermination *(SB994.R15)*
  – Feeding and feeds
  – Juvenile literature
  – Physiology
Rabbits (in religion, folk-lore, etc.)
  See Hares (in religion, folk-lore, etc.)
Rabies
  sa Venom – Physiological effect
  x Hydrophobia
    Lyssa
  – Diagnosis
  – Preventive inoculation
    Example under Inoculation; *and
      under reference from*
      Preventive inoculation
Rabitz construction *(TH1087)*
  xx Building
    Plastering
    Walls
Raccoon hunting
  See Coon hunting
Raccoons *(QL737.C2)*
  sa Coon hunting
  – Juvenile literature
  – Legends and stories *(QL795.R15)*
Race *(Anthropology, GN; Civilization,
  CB195-281; Psychology, BF730-
  738; Sociology, HT1501-1595;
  Theology, BT734)*
  sa Caucasian race
    Ethnic types
    Ethnocentrism
    Mongols
    Negroes
    Occupations and race
  xx Ethnic types
  – Outlines, syllabi, etc.
Race and art
  See Art and race
Race and music
  See Music and race
Race and occupations
  See Occupations and race
Race awareness *(Child study,
  BF723.R3)*
  xx Awareness
    Ethnopsychology
    Intercultural education
    Prejudices and antipathies
    Race problems
Race discrimination *(Direct)*
    Here are entered works dealing with social or
    economic discrimination against racial or
    ethnic groups. Works relating to a
    particular group are entered under the
    name of that group, e.g. Jews – Legal status,
    laws, etc.; Mexicans in the U.S.; Negroes –
    Civil rights. Works on discrimination in
    employment are entered under the heading
    Discrimination in employment or headings
    referred to under this subject.
  sa Discrimination in employment
    Discrimination in housing
    Segregation
  x Anti-discrimination laws
    Discrimination, Racial
    Racial discrimination
  xx Discrimination
    Minorities
    Race problems
    Social problems
  – Law and legislation *(Direct)*
    xx Civil rights
      Equality before the law

Race horses
  sa Thoroughbred horse
  also names of individual race horses
  xx Horse-racing
    Horses
Race improvement
  See Eugenics
    Euthenics
Race problems *(HT1501-1595)*
  sa Acculturation
    Antisemitism
    Church and race problems
    Discrimination
    Emigration and immigration
    Genocide
    Integrated churches
    Intercultural education
    Minorities
    Race awareness
    Race discrimination
    Social service and race problems
    Yellow peril
  also subdivision Native races *under
    names of continents and
    countries, e.g.* Africa – Native
    races; *and subdivision* Race
    question *under names of
    countries, states, cities, etc., e.g.*
    U.S. – Race question; Los
    Angeles – Race question
  x Integration, Racial
    Race question
  xx Assimilation (Sociology)
    Culture conflict
    Ethnology
    History
    Minorities
    Native races
    Negro race
    Social problems
    Sociology
  – Research
Race problems and social service
  See Social service and race problems
Race problems and the church
  See Church and race problems
Race problems in literature
Race psychology
  See Ethnopsychology
Race question
  See Race problems
Racemic acid
  See Tartaric acid
Racemization *(QD501)*
Races of man
  See Ethnology
Rachitis
  See Rickets
Racial amalgamation
  See Miscegenation
Racial crossing
  See Miscegenation
Racial discrimination
  See Race discrimination
Racing *(GV1018)*
  sa Aeroplane racing
    Automobile racing
    Bicycle racing
    Dog racing
    Horse-racing
    Hurdle-racing
    Motor-boat racing
    Motorcycle racing
    Pigeon racing
    Running
    Soap box derbies
    Yacht racing

FIG. 6

Look at another example. The subject you want to research but feel is too broad is rabbits. Figure 6 illustrates the SHLC reference to rabbits.

The subject *rabbits*, then, becomes either broader or narrower depending on how you choose to use the direct and indirect headings.

Section 6 is not an attempt to teach you all there is to know about the book *Subject Headings Used in the Dictionary Catalogs of the Library of Congress.* Its purpose is to introduce you to several ways in which the book can help you. Use it and you will find out how valuable a tool it can be.

Answer 6
Eight *is correct.*

There is a book located in the library entitled *Subject Headings Used in the Dictionary Catalogs of the Library of Congress* (*SHLC*). It is a large book similar to an unabridged dictionary in size. The book contains thousands of subject headings, filed alphabetically, and listings much like a "see" or "see also" card in the card catalog. If you were looking for a particular subject heading in the card catalog but found no such heading on file, you could look up the heading in *SHLC* and it would direct you to the subject heading you could refer to. A sample page from *SHLC* is shown in the Program section on page 90.

The book has other uses. Under each of its main subject headings is a list of subheadings. Under the main subject heading *Transportation,* there are many subheadings—such as *air travel, automobiles,* and *bridges.* Each of these subheadings is a separate subject heading that you could look up in the card catalog.

Notice the "*sa*" notation just below the main *Transportation* heading. The "*sa*" means "see also," and all the subheadings under it are good subject headings to refer to for further information.

Notice that "*x*" and "*xx*" notations indicated. The "*x*" notation indicates a subject heading that, if looked up, would only refer you back to *Transportation* again. The "*xx*" notation means that all the headings under it are good, but they are less-related subject headings.

Find the dash that has been marked. A *dash* subheading means that it is a part of the main heading. For the dash indicated, the subheading is "production standards." If you wanted to look up this heading, you would find it under "Transportation—Production Standards."

You can see, then, that this book, *SHLC*, can serve to help you narrow a field of research or to broaden it, depending on the specific use you make of the headings and subheadings.

POSTTEST

LIBRARY CARD CATALOG POSTTEST INSTRUCTIONS

The library card catalog posttest is designed to test your knowledge gained through your study of the Library Card Catalog Workbook. The posttest is very similar to the pretest which you took at the beginning of the text. Follow the directions carefully.

Directions: For each of the following there is only <u>one best</u> answer.

1. To find the card for the book *10 Years Before the Mast,* you would look under
   a. *Years*
   b. the number 10 in the number section of the card catalog
   c. the word *ten* (the number 10 spelled out)
   d. such a title would not have a title card but would, instead, be filed under the author's name or subject heading
   e. I'm not sure

2. Where would the book *10 Boys and a Dog* be filed in the card catalog in relation to the book *11 Fragrant Houseplants?*
   a. before
   b. after
   c. it could be either before or after with the system used at most universities
   d. I'm not sure

3. To find the book *And Many Went Down* in the card catalog, you would look under
   a. *And*
   b. *Many*
   c. either *a* or *b* — cards are filed both ways at most universities
   d. such a title would not have a title card but would, instead, be filed under the author's name or subject heading
   e. I'm not sure

4. The title card for the book *Oneida Community* would be found filed in which tray?
   a. **On c - On the r**
   b. **On the s - one h**
   c. **One i - O'Neill, E**
   d. **O'Neill, F - Oo**
   e. I'm not sure

5. An author card for William John M'Comca would be found in which tray?
   a. **Comb - Comg**
   b. **Mazj - Meaning o**
   c. **M - Macaq**
   d. **Maccom - Maccq**
   e. I'm not sure

6. An author card for James McAstel would be found filed
   a. before McArthur and before MacFarlane
   b. after M'Aberdeen and after MacDougal
   c. before MacAuley and after MacArthur
   d. after MacMellon and before M'Ferson
   e. I'm not sure

7. The title card for the book *America the Beautiful* would be found in which tray?
   a. **Amer - America de**
   b. **America e - Americains**
   c. **American - Amer. Art Assoc**
   d. **Amer. Women - Amerika**
   e. I'm not sure

8. The title card for the book *U.S. History in a Nutshell* would be found filed in which tray?

   a. **U - Umpire**   c. **Urban - Usury**

   b. **Una - Unm**   d. **Ut - Uya**

9. An author card for Charles James Smith-Hughes (Smith-Hughes is a compound last name) would be found in which tray?

   a. **Small - Smith, J**   c. **Hok - Hughes, M**

   b. **Smith, K - Snap**   d. **Hughes, M - Hyatt**

<h2>SECTION 2   CALL NUMBERS</h2>

Directions: For the following questions refer to the sample call number chart on the next page. Choose your answers for all three questions from the single set of choices below. In each case choose the <u>one best</u> answer.

Where would you find the following call numbers?

10) 320.972	11) Whitman	12) Sci Ref
Es 88m	091	638.267
	D 31r	E 120

a. Level 1   c. Level 3   e. Level 5   g. Room 426   i. I'm not

b. Level 2   d. Level 4   f. Room 407   h. M'200 section   sure

                                                       of Level 4

<h2>SECTION 3   CROSS-REFERENCE CARDS</h2>

Directions: Select the <u>one best</u> answer for each of the following questions.

13. Books under the subject heading *Flying Machines - Poetry* are actually filed under the subject heading *Aeronautics - Poetry*. How would you discover this if you did not know?

   a. when you looked up *Flying Machines* you would find a card that said "see Aeronautics"

   b. you would need to consult the reference librarian

   c. you would need to begin checking the cross references on some book concerning Flying Machines and eventually you would run across the heading "Aeronautics"

   d. you would not be able to tell in this case

   e. I'm not sure

14. The subject heading *Cows* has several title cards filed under it in the card catalog. There are other subject headings related to cows that may also be of value — such as *Calves, Dairying,* and *Milk.* How would you learn of these additional subject headings?

   a. when you looked up *Cows* in the card catalog you would find a card that said "see also Calves, Dairying, and Milk."

   b. you would need to consult the reference librarian

   c. you would need to begin checking the cross references on some book related to cows and eventually you would run across the headings *Calves, Dairying, and Milk.*

   d. you would not be able to tell in this case

   e. I'm not sure

Directions: Select the <u>one best</u> answer for each of the following questions.

SECTION 4 AUTHOR, SUBJECT, AND TITLE CARDS

15. The words in red at the top of some library cards indicate
    a. the subject of that card
    b. the title of that card
    c. the author of that card
    d. an additional subject heading or co-author to which you could refer
    e. an additional book title to which you could refer
    f. none of the above
    g. I'm not sure

16. Books *about* an author are filed where in relation to books *by* him?
    a. before
    b. after
    c. in most filing systems, either before or after is acceptable
    d. I'm not sure

17. Books about the subject "bird" (e.g., *The Bird Book*) would be filed where in relation to books by an author named Bird (e.g., James Bird)?
    a. before
    b. after
    c. in most filing systems either before or after is acceptable
    d. I'm not sure

18. Cards with the same subject heading are filed in what order in the card catalog?

    a. alphabetical order according to the first word of the title

    b. alphabetical order according to the author's last name

    c. chronologically according to the date of printing

    d. none of the above

    e. I'm not sure

19. Who is the author?

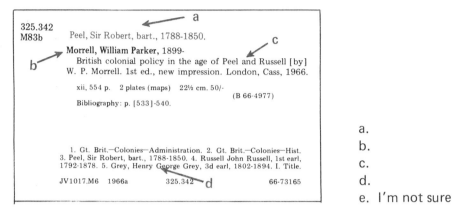

    a.
    b.
    c.
    d.
    e. I'm not sure

20. What is the title?

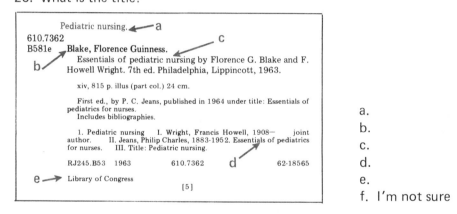

    a.
    b.
    c.
    d.
    e.
    f. I'm not sure

SECTION 5 TRACINGS

21. The tracings on a library card will refer you to additional *book titles* you can look up that are related to the one on that particular card.

    a. true   b. false   c. I'm not sure

22. The tracings on a library card will often refer you to additional *subject headings* you can look under to find books related to the one you are looking for.

    a. true   b. false   c. I'm not sure

23. The arabic numeral(s) in the tracing of a library card are

    a. very important to the student if he is to find further information on his subject

    b. indicate title and/or author cards available on that particular book

    c. both *a* and *b*

    d. I'm not sure

24. The roman numeral(s) in the tracing on a library card
    a. indicate the title and added entry cards that may be available on that particular book
    b. indicate related subject heading cards available
    c. indicate additional *books* available and related to this one
    d. there are no roman numerals in the tracings
    e. I'm not sure

Directions: Each of the following questions deals with the book *Subject Headings Used in the Dictionary Catalogs of the Library of Congress.* **Follow the directions for each one.**

25. Which of the following does the book *SHLC* help you with? (**Mark all correct answers**)
    a. it gives you subject headings not filed in the card catalog
    b. it gives you book titles and their corresponding subject headings not otherwise found in the card catalog
    c. it helps you narrow a field of research to more specific headings
    d. it helps you expand a subject of research to include more and related subjects
    e. it gives a comprehensive list of authors, subject headings, and book titles available in the Library of Congress
    f. I'm not sure

26. A double "*xx*" entry in the book *SHLC* indicates (**Choose <u>the best</u> answer**)
    a. a heading that will only lead back to the main heading
    b. a good but less-related heading
    c. the best heading to look up for related information
    d. a subject heading with books by the same name
    e. a heading that is not filed as listed — indicating that you must refer to another reference book for the correct listing
    f. I'm not sure

27. A single "*x*" entry indicates (**Choose <u>the best</u> answer**)
    a. a heading that will only lead back to the main heading
    b. a good but less-related heading
    c. the best heading to look up for related information
    d. a subject heading with books by the same name
    e. a heading that is not filed as listed — indicating that you must refer to another reference book for the correct listing
    f. I'm not sure

28. An "*sa*" entry indicates (**Choose <u>the best</u> answer**)
    a. an article in the journal "Scientific American"
    b. a "series of articles" are available in various journals
    c. a "scientific article" only
    d. a "social-science article" only
    e. "see also"
    f. I'm not sure

Section 1
1 - c
2 - b
3 - a
4 - c
5 - d
6 - c
7 - b
8 - b
9 - b

Section 2
10 - a
11 - f
12 - b

Section 3
13 - a
14 - a

Section 4
15 - a
16 - b
17 - b
18 - b
19 - b
20 - c

Section 5
21 - b
22 - a
23 - a
24 - a

Section 6
25 - a, c, d
26 - b
27 - a
28 - e